Developing Literacy Using Reading Manipulatives

WRITTEN BY

Sandi Hill

CONTRIBUTING WRITERS

Mary Kurth
Joellyn Thrall Cicciarelli

EDITOR

Joellyn Thrall Cicciarelli

PROJECT DIRECTOR

Carolea Williams

ILLUSTRATOR

Jane Yamada

Table of Contents

Introduction 3

(WORKING WITH ORAL LANGUAGE) 5

Featured Reading Manipulatives 6
Poems, Chants, Stories, Nursery Rhymes 8
Games, Movement 11
Drama, Creative Play, Music 14
Connection with Writing 17
Imagination, Personal Experiences 20

(WORKING WITH LETTERS) 23

Featured Reading Manipulatives 24
Link Letters to Known Words and Names 26
Sort, Classify 29
ABC Books, Songs, Rhymes, Chants 32
Connection with Words in Print 35
Letter Walls, Word Walls, Word Banks 38

(WORKING WITH WORDS) 41

Featured Reading Manipulatives 42
Build Words 44
Break Down Words 47
Prior Knowledge, Context Clues, Picture Clues 50
Vocabulary Games, Literature-Based Activities 53
Spelling Games, Word Comparisons, Writing 56

(WORKING WITH SENTENCES) 59

Featured Reading Manipulatives 60
Build Sentences 62
Punctuation Demonstrations, Sorting Games 65
Hide-and-Seek, Guessing Games, Dramatic Play 68
Break Sentences into Parts 71
Reading-Strategy Games, Literature-Based Activities 74

(WORKING WITH TEXT) 77

Featured Reading Manipulatives 78
Prediction, Prior Knowledge 80
"Play with" Sentences, Punctuation, and Print 83
Visual Aids 86
Work with and Create Text 89
Finger Plays, Oral Presentations 92

Incorporating manipulatives into a reading program is based on the philosophy that active involvement with concrete materials is essential for learning, a philosophy that mathematics and science teachers have known and prescribed to for years.

Many teachers are eager to teach reading using manipulatives, but have been limited to manipulatives for individual, out-of-context letters and words unconnected to "real life" or literature. *Developing Literacy Using Reading Manipulatives* gives you more—it shows children how to connect letters, words, and sentences with literature or child-created text and physically work with them so children can create meaning and understand print.

WORKING WITH THE CHAPTERS Read through each chapter before choosing reading skills on which to concentrate. The skills presented increase in complexity from chapter to chapter. When choosing chapter concentration, consider the developmental level of your students. For example, kindergarten teachers will probably use all activities in Chapter Two (Working with Letters) and some in Chapter Five (Working with Text). Second-grade teachers will probably use all activities in Chapter Five and some in Chapter Two.

TEACHING STRATEGIES Each chapter presents five general teaching strategies to develop oral, letter, word, sentence, or text skills. The strategies are presented in a broad-based context so you have a wide variety of activities from which to choose. The strategies are designed to help you incorporate manipulative activities that generate creativity, curiosity, experimentation, and imagination in reading, all vital qualities in the development of problem-solving, critical-thinking, and most importantly, literacy skills.

READING MANIPULATIVES Children are active learners and must be given opportunities to "play with" print. Working with manipulatives gives children the perfect opportunity to become engaged in learning, becoming more than mere listeners and observers.

Reading manipulatives reinforce children's understanding of reading strategies. With this approach to reading, children have fun while being immersed in print. Learning is enhanced because children see, touch, feel, and move letters, words, sentences, and text.

As children explore and work with reading manipulatives, you will observe and discover what they know about print while assessing abilities. Skills can be presented in any order so you can guide children at their own developmental levels. Activities using manipulatives offer opportunities for reinforcement because they remain exciting and seem "new" even after dozens of experiences.

Two illustrated pages of reading manipulatives are presented for each chapter. These manipulatives are page-referenced in each activity's materials list. Other more common manipulatives are not illustrated—they are probably already in your classroom or are easily made. Make substitutions as necessary if manipulatives are unavailable or cannot be made.

ACTIVITIES Each activity includes a materials list, explanation, and illustration. To integrate the activities into your reading program, all letters, words, sentences, and text used should be generated from "real" literature (either published or student-generated) and your curriculum guidelines.

When planning activities, decide if they are best suited for working with individuals, small groups, or the whole class. At first, use activities that are simple in nature, progressing to more challenging activities as children become proficient. Activities can be taught as lessons in a unit or as mini-lessons—adapt them to fit the various learning styles in your class.

Many activities include a recording component so children have one more way to express their learning. Depending on children's developmental levels, recording can be modified into writing or drawing. Have children record often—it is a window into their thinking.

After completing an activity, place the manipulatives in a learning center. Invite children to explore the manipulatives to complete the same activity or one of their own. Children love to play with favorite manipulatives again and again. When you recognize favorite manipulatives, think of other reading activities and incorporate them into your reading program.

REPRODUCIBLES Many activities have reproducibles that become reading manipulatives when used in pocket charts, graphs, or games. To preserve reproducibles for multiple use, glue them to construction paper, laminate, and cut them apart.

WORKING WITH Oral Language

Developing phonemic awareness through oral language is the first step in laying the foundation for children's reading instruction. There is a strong link between children's reading success and the development of phonemic awareness taught through oral language.

READING SKILLS

Working with oral language develops the following reading skills. Children who understand and can work with oral language:

- recognize letters by their names and sounds.
- understand we speak in a flow of words.
- know words are composed of a limited number of sounds.
- understand word/sound correspondence.
- use rhythm, rhyme, and repetition to remember words and sentences.
- understand how listening, speaking, reading, and writing are connected.
- develop listening skills.
- can follow directions.
- orally relay information and answer questions.

TEACHING STRATEGIES

The following teaching strategies offer unique ways to help children gain oral language skills. Pages 8 through 22 provide dozens of oral language activities. Each activity incorporates reading manipulatives and one of these teaching strategies.

- Use poems, chants, stories, and nursery rhymes in a variety of ways.
- Play games and use movement.
- Have children participate in drama, creative play, or musical activities.
- Use writing in a variety of ways to show the connection between oral language and print.
- Invite children to use their imagination or draw from personal experiences to communicate ideas orally.

READING MANIPULATIVES

Pages 6 and 7 show several reading manipulatives featured in this and other chapters. Consult these pages when making manipulatives, when deciding which manipulatives to use, and to determine possible substitutions.

Featured Reading Manipulatives

Noisemakers

maracas   jingle bells   cans filled with rice   tambour-ines   whistles   rhythm sticks

Rubber Stamp Letters

Action Cards

On posterboard (large cards) or index cards (small cards) write an action that begins with each letter of the alphabet, such as **a**im, **b**ounce, **c**rawl, **d**ance, **e**at, **f**all, **g**allop, **h**op, **i**ce skate, **j**og, **k**ick, **l**augh, **m**unch, **n**ap, **o**perate, **p**unch, **q**uestion, **r**ide a bike, **s**tir, **t**alk, use a **u**kulele, **v**acuum, **w**ash, e**x**amine, **y**awn, and **z**ip. Write the beginning letter of each word on the other side.

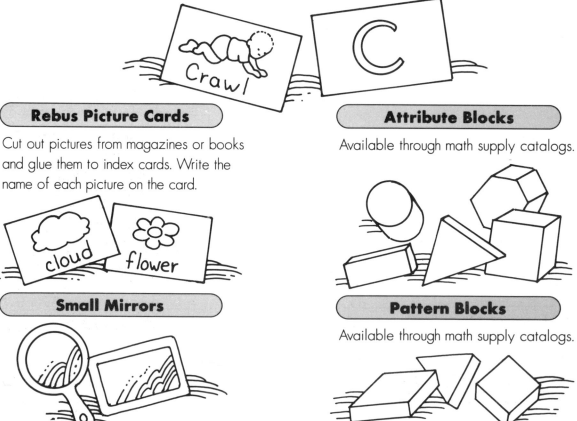

Rebus Picture Cards

Cut out pictures from magazines or books and glue them to index cards. Write the name of each picture on the card.

Attribute Blocks

Available through math supply catalogs.

Small Mirrors

Pattern Blocks

Available through math supply catalogs.

Featured Reading Manipulatives

Costume Trunk

Prop Trunk

Magnet Boards

cookie sheets

magnetic boards

oil drip pans from auto supply

Phonics Phones

Plumbers' PVC elbow pipes.

Puppets

sock puppets

paper-bag puppets

purchased puppets

Plastic Chain Links

How Big Is It?

MATERIALS

LinkerCubes
(see page 24)

emergent reader

index cards

markers

Choose several short, medium, and long words from an emergent reader and write them on index cards. Tell the class that sometimes you can tell if a word is short, medium, or long just by listening to it. Give specific examples such as *is, smile,* and *demonstration.* Invite children to listen and look for short, medium, and long words in the reader as you read it aloud. (Read slowly but fluently, pointing to each word as you say it.) Distribute LinkerCubes or Unifix cubes. Tell children you will say a word and they should build a short, medium, or long cube stack depending on the length of the word. (For example, if you say the word *he,* children should build a two- or three-cube stack. If you say, *congratulations,* children should build a nine- or ten-cube stack.) Say each word, giving children time to build. Show each word, circulating the room and having children make adjustments. To guide students, ask questions such as *Did you hear me talk for a long time or a short time when I said _____? Look at the letters. How can you tell it is a long/medium/short word?*

Hearing Sentences

MATERIALS

emergent reader

sentence strips

markers

small paper treat cups

raisins, M&Ms, or oyster crackers

Write several short sentences from an emergent reader on sentence strips. Write a sentence from the book on the board. Read the sentence and point out the punctuation. Invite children to count the number of words in the sentence by holding up their fingers as you read. Read the emergent reader aloud, pointing to words as you read. Distribute paper cups and treats. Slowly read a sentence strip. Have children count the number of words in the sentence, placing a treat in their cups each time they hear a word. Show the sentence, inviting a volunteer to come up and count the words. Have children count the number of treats they placed in their cups to check if they counted correctly. After children have counted the words in all the sentences, invite them to eat their treats.

In advance, write each line of *Jack and Jill* on a sentence strip. Write the rhyming words, *Jill, hill, down,* and *crown* in red marker. Write the rest of the words in green. Write another nursery rhyme such as *Little Miss Muffet* in black marker. Display *Jack and Jill* in the pocket chart. Read the rhyme aloud, pointing to each word as you say it. Talk about the rhyming words, how they look and sound the same and where they are on the lines. Distribute noisemakers. Read the nursery rhyme several times, inviting the class to use their noisemakers when you read each rhyming word. Collect the noisemakers. Display the other rhyme in the pocket chart. Read the rhyme aloud. Tell children the number of rhyming words in the rhyme and challenge them to listen for and find them. Read the rhyme several times, asking children to raise their hands when they think they have found all rhyming words. Redistribute the noisemakers. Read the rhyme again, inviting the class to use noisemakers when you read each rhyming word. Continue reading until most of the class makes noise during the rhyming words. Reveal the rhyming words. To close, invite the class to make noise when you read every word.

MATERIALS

sentence strips

red, green, and black markers

pocket chart

noisemakers (see page 6)

Photocopy the Tongue Twisters reproducible and 13 Book Page reproducibles for each child. Cut the book pages in half and make 26-page blank books. Teach one tongue twister a week. Each day, distribute blank books and have children recite the assigned tongue twister several times. All week, have children use one book page and make a page border by stamping the tongue twister's letter once each time they recite it. For example, if the class recites the tongue twister ten times, they would stamp the letter ten times. At the end of the week, count stamped letters so children know how many times they said the tongue twister. Invite each child to write the assigned tongue twister on the book page and illustrate its meaning. Continue through the alphabet.

Twist My Tongue!

MATERIALS

Tongue Twisters reproducible (page 95)

Book Page reproducible (page 96)

stapler

rubber stamp letters (see page 6)

ink pads

Jump-Rope Fun

MATERIALS

Jump-Rope Rhyme reproducible
(page 97)

long jump rope

Reproduce and distribute the Jump-Rope Rhyme. Teach the Jump-Rope Rhyme by reading it aloud, having children repeat lines after you, and then read aloud with you. Show children how to swing a jump rope low to the ground from left to right, without twirling it overhead. Demonstrate how to jump. (If children have difficulty jumping a swinging rope, lay an outstretched rope on the ground and have children jump over it from left to right.) Invite a few children to jump the rope while the rest of the class recites the Jump-Rope Rhyme. Throughout the year, teach other jump-rope rhymes, and have the class take turns jumping.

Teddy bear,
Teddy bear...

Eating Sounds

MATERIALS

emergent reader

index cards

markers

small paper treat cups

masking tape

raisins, M&Ms, or oyster crackers

Choose several words from an easy reader that contain the same sound. Write each word on an index card, highlighting the sound's letter or letter combination with a different-colored marker. Use masking tape to label three cups for each child. Label the first cup *beginning,* the second *middle,* and the third *end.* Read the reader aloud. Distribute three cups and a handful of treats to each child. Tell children you are going to say a series of words that contain the same sound, such as /p/. Tell children they should listen for the sound at the beginning, middle, or end of the word. Read a word from an index card without showing it to the class. Invite children to place a treat in the *beginning* cup if they hear the sound at the beginning of the word, the *middle* cup if they hear the sound in the middle, and the *end* cup if they hear the sound at the end. Show and read the word card, have the class repeat it, and point out the sound placement. Invite children to check their cups to see if they placed the treat in the correct place. Invite children to remove and eat their treats. At the end of the game, have children eat the leftovers.

Play this game in an open area. Have children stand in a large circle. To model, distribute an action card to each child. Invite each child to hold up his or her card, show and say the name of the letter, and demonstrate the action that goes with it. Explain that you will randomly call out letter names (or sounds). When a child recognizes his or her letter, he or she holds up his or her action word, signaling for the class to perform the action. The class then performs the action until you call out another letter. When you call out a new letter, all children quit their performance, return to the circle, and display their cards if they match the letter called. Play the game until the entire alphabet has been called.

Alphabet Actions

MATERIALS

action cards (see page 6)

Distribute mirrors. Using a picture book, read aloud one word for each letter of the alphabet. For each letter, invite children to look in the mirror, say the word represented by the letter, and then say the word's beginning sound several times. For example, have children say *cat, /c/, /c/, /c/.* When children say the sound, point out teeth, tongue, and mouth positions. Next, invite children to hold mirrors for partners. Have children say the letters again and place their hands in front of their mouths as they speak, feeling the air expel. Finally, have children say the letters and place their hands on their chins to feel mouth position. Extension: Invite a speech pathologist to perform a related lesson with the whole class. (It will do wonders for speech students' self-esteem.)

Seeing Sounds

MATERIALS

picture book

small mirrors (see page 6)

Simon Says

MATERIALS

tangible letters (see page 24)

Divide the class into pairs. Distribute one set of tangible letters to each pair. Play Simon Says by using commands such as *Simon says, touch the letter F with your pinky. Simon says, place the letter that sounds like /p/ on the floor. Place the J and Q on your shoe.* When eliminating pairs that perform a command incorrectly, invite them to sit near you and think of commands for the class.

Can You Guess?

MATERIALS

rebus picture cards (see page 6)

paper bag

alphabet chart

Place picture cards in a paper bag. Invite a volunteer to choose a picture card and describe the object on the card without saying its name. Have children raise their hands and guess the name of the object. Invite the child who guessed the object's name to take the rebus card and describe the first letter of the object's name. For example, if the child correctly guessed *horse,* he or she might say, *The first letter has a stick and a hump. The hump is on the bottom of the stick.* Invite children to consult the alphabet chart and guess the letter's name. Have the child who guessed the letter's name choose a new card and describe the object.

Work with a small group. Place attribute blocks in a paper bag. Pass the bag to a child and have him or her reach in and pull out five attribute blocks. Demonstrate how to sort the blocks. Sort them into as many groups as you wish—by thickness, shape, or color. Place the blocks back in the bag. Invite the child to choose again. Invite him or her to sort the new blocks, calling on friends for help if he or she wishes. Ask the child to explain how he or she sorted. Have each child take a turn and give an oral explanation.

Attribute Sort

MATERIALS

attribute blocks (see page 6)

paper bag

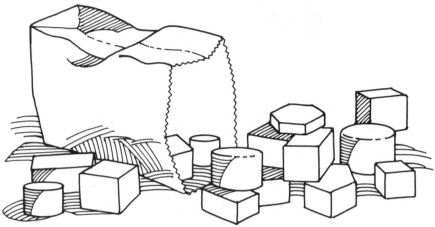

In advance, build a simple tessellation or pattern with pattern blocks inside a cardboard box. Divide the class into groups. Distribute pattern blocks to each group. For each group, assign an observer and a messenger; the rest of the group will be builders. Have observers come to the box and look inside. Ask observers to explain what the blocks look like to the messengers. Ask the messengers to relay the information back to his or her group so they can begin making what they understand the blocks look like. (The observer should not be able to see what builders are doing.) If the builders have questions, they must ask the messenger to relay the questions to the observer. Have each group make their interpretation of the directions. After all groups finish, have them display their creations and discuss the similarities and differences before displaying the original blocks. Invite children to discuss the importance of clearly stating ideas and directions.

What Do We Do?

MATERIALS

pattern blocks (see page 6)

cardboard box

Add a triangle.

Letter Charades

MATERIALS

action cards (page 6)

hat

Place small action cards in a hat. Have a volunteer choose a card and perform the action. Invite children to raise their hands and guess the action and the name of the letter the volunteer is acting out.

Silly Sentences

MATERIALS

paper bag

small toys and objects

For each child, place one small toy or object in a paper bag. Objects could include a small toy car, doll, pencil, rock, house, or airplane. Have the class sit in a large circle. Ask a child to choose an object from the bag without looking. Have the child make up a silly sentence using the name of the chosen object. For example, if a child chooses a toy airplane, he or she might say, *One day Godzilla got so hungry, he went to the airport and ate an airplane.* After the child says a sentence, have him or her pass the bag to the next child. Continue passing the bag until everyone has a turn.

Read aloud a favorite story. Divide the class into groups. Have groups make up and practice a skit to dramatize the story. Before performing, invite each group to use the costume and prop trunks and dress up for the performance. Have each group perform their skit for the class. After the performances, discuss the skits' similarities and differences.

Show the Story

MATERIALS

read-aloud picture book

costume and prop trunks
(see page 7)

Photocopy and distribute Hokey Pokey reproducibles. Have children cut out the body-part cards. Ask children to sit on the floor in a large circle and place the cards, in random order, face up in front of them. Invite half the class to come to the center of the circle, forming a smaller circle facing out toward the children sitting on the floor. Play "The Hokey Pokey." Invite children sitting to find and hold up a body-part card when they hear the word in the song. (These children hold up clues for the children in the center.) Have children in the center dance "The Hokey Pokey," watching for help from the sitting children. When the song is over, switch groups and repeat the activity.

Hokey-Pokey Picture Play

MATERIALS

Hokey Pokey reproducible (page 98)

scissors

"The Hokey Pokey" on record or cassette

record or tape player

Change the Story

MATERIALS

emergent reader, two copies

scissors

felt strips

felt board

glue

In advance, cut pictures of characters, places, and objects from an emergent reader. Laminate the pictures and glue a felt strip to the back of each. Read the other copy of the reader aloud. Have children discuss the story and name the characters. Place their pictures on the felt board. Ask children to name places from the story. Display the place pictures on the board. Then ask children to name objects from the story and place the object pictures on the board. Invite each child to use his or her imagination and create a new story using the same characters, places, and objects. Place the felt board in a learning center. Give children time each day for a week to play with the pieces and create a story. At the end of the week, invite each child to manipulate the pieces as he or she tells a new story.

Telephone Conversations

MATERIALS

read-aloud picture book

two toy telephones

Read aloud a favorite picture book. To discuss the story, have telephone conversations with students. Choose a volunteer. Using a toy telephone, have the volunteer dial your number. (Write any phone number on the board.) Make a ringing sound and pick up a second telephone. Have the volunteer use a common telephone greeting such as *Is Mrs. Garcia there?* and begin a conversation with you. Speak as if you are on the telephone, asking the child about the book, and inviting him or her to share information. After a short conversation, tell the child you have to go, say *good-bye*, and hang up the phone. Invite each child to call you and discuss the book.

Distribute plastic lids, marking pens, and damp paper towels. Invite a volunteer to choose three rebus picture cards. Ask him or her to say a word from one of the cards, speaking slowly, clearly, and with projection. Ask the class to listen carefully to the word, write the first letter they hear on their plastic lids, and "flip" their lids to show their answers. Ask the volunteer to show the card so children can check their answers. Have children erase letters with damp towels in preparation for the next word. Continue the activity with several volunteers. Extension: Have children listen for ending or middle letters or for all letters they can hear.

Flip Your Lids

MATERIALS

round plastic lids

Vis-a-Vis marking pens

damp paper towels

rebus picture cards (see page 6)

Working with a small group, read aloud a picture book. Have the group brainstorm favorite words from the story. List the words on chart paper. Invite children to repeat the words after you read them aloud, read them aloud with you, and finally, read them alone. Ask each child to choose his or her favorite word from the list and make that word using shoelaces. After words are made, have children read their word to the group and tell why they chose them.

Favorite Words

MATERIALS

read-aloud picture book

chart paper

markers

shoelaces

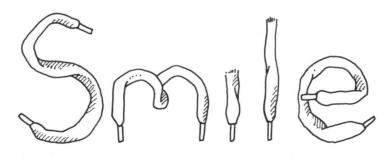

Color Chants

MATERIALS

Color Chants reproducibles
(pages 99–111)

Other Ways to Use Color Chants
reproducible (page 112)

construction paper

glue

magnetic tape

magnet boards (see page 7)

Enlarge and reproduce Color Chants and signs, glue each to a piece of construction paper that corresponds with the color, and laminate them. Cut out the words and signs and place magnetic tape on the back of each. Arrange each chant on a magnet board. Each time you introduce or study a color, have children learn a color chant. Introduce the chant, reading it aloud and pointing to each word as you say it. Invite the class to read the chant aloud with you. Then, have the class echo each line back to you after you read it. Have the class read the chant themselves. Mix up the words in the first line. Invite the class to tell how to arrange them in order and read it to you. Repeat this procedure with each line. Mix up all the words, inviting the class to put them in order and read it back to you. After children have learned the chant, teach them the signs that go with each word. Have children repeat the chant while performing the signs. For other color-chant activities, see page 112.

Phonics Phone

MATERIALS

phonics phones (see page 7)

writing paper

pencils

Help children make a connection between sounds and writing with this activity. Whenever students are writing, give them a phonics phone. Have children put the phone to their ear and mouth, and slowly say the word they want to write several times. (The word's sound goes directly into the child's ear and is not "lost" in the air.) Ask each child to lay down the phone, write the word, and use the phone for each subsequent word.

In advance, copy a favorite rhyming poem on chart paper, highlighting rhyming word pairs with different-colored markers. Glue a Rhyming Pairs reproducible to construction paper. Laminate the construction paper and cut out the words. Discuss rhyming words. Read aloud a favorite rhyming poem, pointing out the rhyming words. Mix up and display the rhyming pair cards. Invite children to listen to each word as you read it aloud, find its pair, and join the pair with a clothespin. Give each child a turn to find a word match. When all matches are found, have children read the pairs aloud.

In advance, copy the following sentences on sentence strips: *One day some ____1____ went to a ____2____. To their surprise, a ____3____ fell on their car. To get home, they rode a ____4____.* Reproduce Fill the Blank and cut out the words. Glue each word to an index card and divide the cards into four sets according to their number. Place each set in a container. Display the sentence strips in a pocket chart and read them aloud. Tell children the story's meaning will change when different words are used in each blank. Invite four volunteers to choose words from each container. Place the words in their correct place in the chart. Read the story aloud and discuss it. Invite four more children to choose cards and place them in the chart. Invite children to read the new story with you. Repeat the activity with every card. When all stories have been read, have children think of their own words to add to the story. Write them on index cards, place them in the chart, and read the children's story.

Rhyming Pairs

MATERIALS

chart paper

markers

Rhyming Pairs reproducible (page 113)

construction paper

glue

favorite rhyming poem

clothespins

Fill the Blank

MATERIALS

sentence strips

markers

Fill the Blank reproducible (page 114)

index cards

glue

four containers

pocket chart

A My Name Is Amy

MATERIALS

colored chalk

tangible letters (see page 24)

container

Write the words *Name, Friend, Place,* and *Action* on the board. Under the words, write the appropriate phrases—*A my name is Amy, and my friend's name is Alex. We come from Alaska, and we eat apples.* Read the sentences aloud, pointing to words as you read. Invite volunteers to find the names of the girl, her friend, the place, and what they do. Have volunteers use colored chalk to circle the first letter of each word *(A).* Have the class sit in a large circle on the floor. Pass a container of tangible letters, and have each child take one. Ask each child to use the letter and think of sentences with new words for *Amy, Alex, Alaska,* and *apples.* For example, *B my name is Betty, and my friend's name is Bernardo. We come from Bombay, and we ride bikes.* Give children time to think, walking around the circle to help, if needed. Invite children to share their sentences. Extension: Copy each child's sentence on construction paper and have him or her illustrate it.

Tell Me, Tell Them

MATERIALS

puppets (see page 7)

Have each child find a partner. Distribute a puppet to each child. Have children think of a favorite personal story, such as a story about a vacation, holiday, or funny event. Invite one child from each pair to put on a puppet and tell his or her story to the other child's puppet. Have children who heard the stories wear their puppets and retell the stories to the class. Have children trade roles and repeat the activity. Children not only practice sharing new ideas, they practice listening and relaying information.

Tell children that a story is a chain of ideas. Distribute a plastic or paper chain link to each child. Have the class sit in a circle on the floor. Holding up your chain link, start telling a story with one sentence, such as *One summer night, Jesse and Tasha decided to go for a walk through the woods.* (Be sure to establish setting and characters in your sentence.) Pass your link to the child on your left. Ask that child to add to your story with a new sentence. Encourage the child to use his or her imagination so the story becomes interesting. After the child adds a sentence, have him or her join the two chain links and pass them to the child on the left. Have children continue adding to the story, collecting and linking the chain, and passing the chain until it comes back to you. When you receive the chain, make up and tell an ending for the story.

Story Add-On

MATERIALS

plastic chain links (see page 7)

Write numbers on slips of paper. Take each child outside the room, one at a time, away from the rest of the class. Give the first child a number one paper slip, the second a number two, and so on. On writing paper, record each child's name next to his or her number. Have each child speak into the tape recorder and tell you his or her number and then something he or she likes about school. After the tape is complete, return to the classroom. Invite the class to listen to each person on the tape. Stop the tape after each child speaks. Ask the class to guess who is speaking, then invite the speaker to reveal him or herself. Ask children if they recognize their own voices. Invite children to discuss how it feels to hear their and others' voices.

Guess That Voice

MATERIALS

paper slips

writing paper

pencil

tape recorder

blank cassette tape

Field-Trip Fun

MATERIALS

die-cut letters
(see page 24)

paper bag

drawing paper

glue

crayons, markers

class book-binding materials
and cover

Before a field trip, have the class brainstorm what they might see that begins with each letter of the alphabet. For example, if the class is going to the zoo, children might say they will see an anteater, bear, cougar, and so on. During the trip, have children point out items that begin with each letter. After the trip, have the class sit in a large circle. Have each child choose a letter from a paper bag. Invite each child to think of one thing he or she saw or did on the field trip that started with his or her letter. For example, if a child has an A, he or she might choose to talk about an antelope at the zoo. (If you wish, do not put infrequently-used letters in the bag.) Go around the circle, helping children think of something that begins with their letters. Have each child take a turn holding up and naming his or her letter and reporting a sight or action. Have children go to their seats and glue their letters to drawing paper. Near the letter, have each child draw a picture of his or her sight or action. Collect papers and bind them into a class book.

Name That Word!

MATERIALS

index cards

markers

read-aloud picture book

In advance, write several key words from a read-aloud picture book on index cards. Words can include character names, important places, and verbs that describe story actions. Read the book aloud. Tell students you have word cards that tell about the story. Invite volunteers to retell the story. Whenever a volunteer says one of the written words, display the word on the chalk rail and have the class say the word. Continue retelling and repeating until all cards have been displayed. If you have leftover cards, ask questions to elicit responses that use the words.

WORKING WITH Letters

To continue building a strong foundation for reading, letter knowledge is essential to construct meaning from written words and to work with print. Mastery of letter knowledge includes the ability to name letters, write letters, and use letter sounds as cues when reading and writing. Children should explore letters, letter sounds, attributes of letters, and concepts of print. When teachers model strategies and children have time to practice, working with letters becomes a problem-solving strategy when making sense of print.

READING SKILLS

Working with letters develops the following reading skills. Children who understand and can work with letters:

- know letter names.
- identify upper- and lowercase letters in print.
- match upper- and lowercase letters.
- recognize letter/sound correspondence.
- master letter formation.
- sequence letters of the alphabet.
- locate letters at the beginning of words.
- locate letters in text.
- distinguish between letters and words.

TEACHING STRATEGIES

The following teaching strategies offer unique ways to help children gain letter knowledge. Pages 26 through 40 provide dozens of letter activities. Each activity incorporates the use of reading manipulatives and one of these teaching strategies.

- Link letters to known words and names.
- Sort and classify letters by comparing attributes such as size and shape.
- Read aloud and make alphabet books, sing ABC songs, and repeat or create ABC rhymes and chants.
- Show the connection between letters and words in print.
- Use letter walls, word walls, and word banks.

READING MANIPULATIVES

Pages 24 and 25 show several reading manipulatives featured in this and other chapters. Consult these pages when making manipulatives, when deciding which manipulatives to use, and to determine possible substitutions.

Featured Reading Manipulatives

Tangible Letters

letter cards
Write letters on index or old business cards.

one-inch ceramic or construction-paper letter tiles
Use a paint pen or Sharpie to print letters.

magnetic letters
Have children work on magnet boards (see page 7).

die-cuts
Use Ellison dies or bulletin-board letters.

alphabet cereal, pretzels, and pasta

LinkerCubes

Unifix Cubes

Counters

teddy bears

pennies

marbles

small rocks

Wikki-Stix

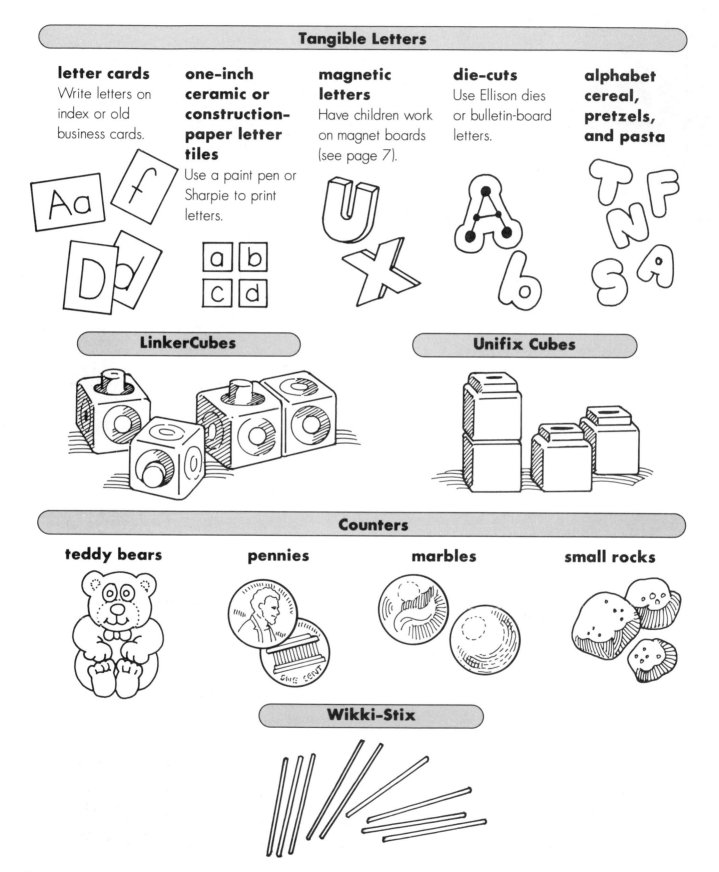

Featured Reading Manipulatives

Name Cards

Write each child's name on an index card. Glue his or her class picture to the card, and laminate.

Alphabet Line

Use plain bulletin-board borders and permanent markers. Write each letter of the alphabet on a border section. Leave six to eight inches between each letter.

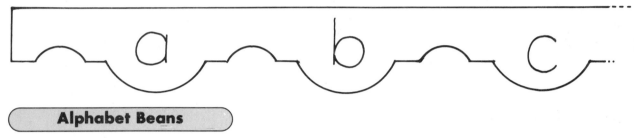

Alphabet Beans

Using permanent marker, write an uppercase letter on a large, plastic or dry, kidney-shaped bean. Write corresponding lowercase letters on the other sides of the beans. Store beans in a can with a plastic lid.

Reading Window

Cut a rectangular hole in the center of a sentence strip.

3-M Post-it Tape Flags

Available at office supply stores.

Cuisenaire Rods

Availabe through math supply catalogs.

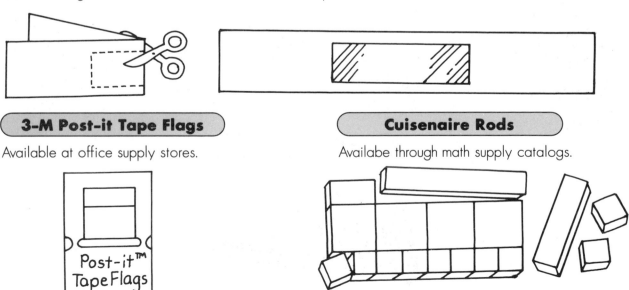

Name-O

MATERIALS

1" (2.5 cm) ceramic or construction-paper letter tiles, three alphabet sets (see page 24)

Name-O Card reproducible (page 115)

name cards (see page 25)

markers

Distribute a Name-O Card to each child. Have children choose four names from name cards and copy each name on a Name-O Card. Children should print one letter in each square, writing each name in a row of its own. (The number of letters in each row is not important.) Turn the letter tiles face down. Have the first player turn over a letter tile and search for that letter on his or her card. If the player finds a match, he or she picks up the tile and places it on top of the letter on the Name-O Card. The player then announces the person's name and the letter it contains, such as, *Jeremy has a Y in his name.* The player draws again if he or she finds a match. If the player does not make a match, he or she turns the tile back over and the game continues with the next player. Continue play until one player covers all of his or her letters and calls out, *Name-O!*

Invitations

MATERIALS

tangible upper- and lowercase letters (see page 24)

name cards (see page 25)

construction paper

markers

scissors

art supplies (glitter, feathers, buttons, tissue paper)

glue

Invite children to choose four name cards, showing names of friends with whom they would like to play at recess. Have children place the name cards in front of them as models and build each name with tangible letters. Ask children to fold a piece of construction paper into fourths and write one name in each quarter. Have children cut the paper into fourths, decorate around the names with art supplies, and present the papers as invitations to play.

Give each child his or her name card and a Measuring Chart. Have each child write his or her name down the left side of the Measuring Chart, one letter in each square (as shown). Ask each child to build his or her name two ways using LinkerCubes or Unifix cubes. First, have children make their names with only the first letter capitalized, then have them make their names in all capital letters. Have each child place the first letter of his or her name on one side of a balance scale. Ask each child to add counters to the other side of the scale until it balances. Ask, *How many counters does the first letter in your name weigh?* Have children record their answers on the Measuring Chart. Invite children to weigh each letter of both names and record their answers. Ask questions such as *Which weighed the most, upper- or lowercase letters? Why do you think one weighed more than the other? Compare the letters in both names—how are they alike and different? How many letters are in your name? Weigh your whole name—how much did it weigh? Build a friend's name that you think weighs the same as yours. Weigh both names—was your guess correct?*

MATERIALS

LinkerCubes or Unifix cubes (see page 24)

name cards (see page 25)

balance scales

counters (see page 24)

Measuring Chart reproducible (page 116)

Give each child a container of macaroni and spaghetti and a Pasta Graph. Invite children to build the letters in their names, using macaroni for the curved lines and spaghetti for the straight lines. Ask them to glue each letter to a separate card. Invite children to observe their letters and record observations (letters that use only macaroni, letters that use only spaghetti, and letters that use both) in the correct columns of the Pasta Graph. To extend the activity, have children make other letters of the alphabet and add to the graph.

Pasta Names

MATERIALS

elbow macaroni

spaghetti

containers

Pasta Graph reproducible (page 117)

old business or index cards

glue

Letter Detective

MATERIALS

big book

Wikki-Stix (see page 24)

After sharing a big book with your class, read the story a second time, having the class chant and read the words with you. Bend a Wikki-Stix into an oval shape by squeezing the ends together. Name and display a letter from the first page of the book and place a Wikki-Stix oval around the letter. Invite a child to come forward and press the Wikki-Stix around the letter. Have the class repeat the letter name. Invite volunteers to find the same letter on other pages of the book and press the oval around it. After the letter has been identified several times, have children identify other letters (or words) from the story and place the oval around them.

Personal Alphabet Books

MATERIALS

28-page, teacher-made blank books

pencils

class lists (first names only)

copies of students' school pictures

scissors

glue

Provide each child with a blank book. Using letters displayed around the room as models, have each child write a letter, in alphabetical order, on each page of his or her book. Distribute class lists. Have children cut out each name on the list and glue it on the appropriate book page according to the first letter of the first name. Invite children to glue classmates' pictures next to the names, and then decorate the first page as a cover. Use the books as personal dictionaries in which students write favorite words or draw pictures of items that start with each letter. Variation: Use the books as class telephone directories, and invite students to write their phone numbers next to their names.

In advance, reproduce and cut out sets of Sorting Rules. Make a set for each student pair. Place each set in a container. Using the Sorting Rules as examples, explain different ways letters can be sorted. Have each child find a partner. Distribute a T-Chart, set of tangible letters, and container of Sorting Rules to each pair. Invite children to place one set of Sorting Rules on top of their T-Chart. Ask children to sort letters by each rule and place the letters in the correct place on the chart. Invite children to test each set of rules, arranging letters on the chart as they go.

Sorting Letters

MATERIALS

Sorting Rules reproducible (page 118)

tangible upper- and lowercase letters (see page 24)

T-Chart reproducible (page 119)

small container

Reproduce the divided-plate illustration. Distribute one scoop of alphabet cereal, a plate, and an illustration of the plate to each child. Invite children to sort the cereal into different categories, placing each category on a different plate section. Students can sort cereal into categories such as letters with dots, letters with sticks, letters with slants, and letters with tails. Invite students to record their findings on the illustration, writing the letters in the sections in which they were placed. Ask questions such as *Which set has the most letters? Which set has the least letters? How many more letters does one set have than another?*

Lunch Tray Sort

MATERIALS

alphabet cereal, pretzels, or pasta (see page 24)

divided paper or foam plates

illustration of divided plate

pencils

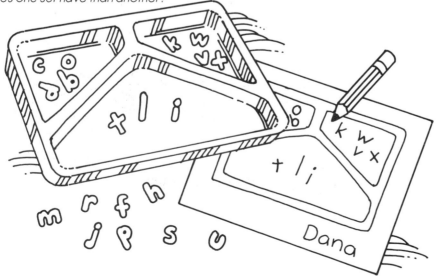

Word Search

MATERIALS

rebus picture cards (see page 6)

alphabet line (see page 25)

pencils

Alphabet Line reproducibles
(pages 120 and 121)

Have children place the alphabet line on the floor. Provide children with rebus picture cards. Have children sort the cards by beginning sound and place them under corresponding letters on the alphabet line. Have children use the reproducible and copy the words under each letter as shown. Extension: Have students sort picture cards, baseball cards, or environmental print by beginning or ending sound and place them under the correct letter on the line.

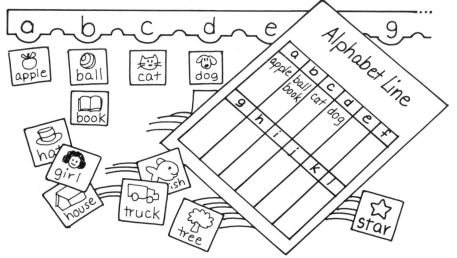

Tricky Letters

MATERIALS

tangible lowercase letters
(see page 24)

two containers, labeled *Container 1*
and *Container 2*

Letter Sets 1 and 2 reproducibles
(pages 122 and 123)

pencils

Place tangible lowercase *Hs, Ns, Ts, Ms, Fs,* and *Ks* in Container 1. Place tangible lowercase *Ps, Qs, Bs, Ds, Gs,* and *Js* in Container 2. Divide children into two groups. Give one group Letter Set and Container 1. Give the other group Letter Set and Container 2. Have children observe the pictures and letters on their reproducibles. Ask children to sort tangible letters and place them on a section of their reproducibles, carefully checking that letters are placed in the correct spaces. A sign of mastery is when children can complete the task quickly and correctly. After letters are sorted, have children write each letter three times in the correct place on their reproducibles. Have groups trade containers. Distribute new reproducibles and have groups complete the task with new letters.

In advance, make one Picky the Puppet. Make signs for Picky that tell what he is being picky about. Each sign should deal with letters of the alphabet, such as *I only like words spelled with five letters; I want pets with Ps in their names; I only like words that start with T; or I only want to look at pictures of things that start with B.* Introduce Picky the Puppet. Explain that Picky got his name when he was very young because he was so picky. Explain that Picky is so picky that every day he changes his mind about what to be picky about. Have children make Picky the Puppet by cutting apart and coloring the reproducible and gluing the pieces to a paper bag. Each day, display one of Picky's signs. Invite children to use resources around the room to find words that meet Picky's requirements. Have children wear their puppets as they point out the letters and words Picky requests.

Have children stamp the alphabet, in order, on adding-machine tape. Invite children to shake a can of alphabet beans, spoon out five letters, and place them in the correct place on the adding-machine tape. Have children shake, scoop, and place beans until the adding-machine tape is filled.

Picky the Puppet

MATERIALS

Picky the Puppet reproducible (page 124)

paper lunch bags

scissors

glue

construction paper

crayons, markers

Letter Cover-Up

MATERIALS

adding-machine tape

rubber stamp letters (see page 6)

ink pads

alphabet beans (see page 25)

can

large spoon

What's My Name? Chant

MATERIALS

index cards

red, blue, green, orange, and black markers

sentence strips

pocket chart

Write each letter of the alphabet on an index card. Write the letters in red, blue, green, and orange markers, creating an easily-seen pattern. Using black marker, print several questions on sentence strips, such as *I am the letter before* M. *What's my name? I am the letter after* S. *What's my name? I am the first letter in* red. *What's my name? I am the letter between* P *and* R. *What's my name?* Place the questions in the top half of the pocket chart. Sequence letter cards (in order) at the bottom of the chart. Read each question, pointing to the words as you read them. Invite children to repeat each sentence after you read it, pointing to the words as children read. Have children read the index-card letters, locate the answers, and report them to the class. Invite volunteers to add sentences to the chart. Write the sentences as volunteers dictate them. Place the new sentences on top of the existing ones and continue the activity.

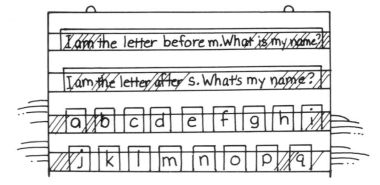

Alphabet Cheer

MATERIALS

die-cut uppercase alphabet (see page 24)

Divide the class into five groups. Distribute five random letters to each group, keeping the letter *A* for yourself. Explain that the class will per- form an "alphabet cheer" by making one of their letters with their bodies each time you shout a sentence. Demonstrate the sentence by shouting, *Give me an* A! Immediately after shouting, form your body into a capital *A* and invite children to cheer, *A!* Explain that they may each form letters individually or use their whole group to make one letter. Tell children they may stand, sit, or lie down to make letters. Invite each group to practice forming their letters. Take the class into an open area and perform the cheer, keeping the letter *A* for yourself. Invite the class to help you shout the cheer. Yell, *Give me a(n) ___ !* for each letter, giving groups time to show their letters while the rest of the class yells the names.

Each day, explore one page of *Animalia* with the class. Invite a volunteer to use the reading window and place it over the featured letter. Choose another child to use the window and locate an item on the page that begins with the featured letter. For example, have one child locate the letter *D* and the other child locate an item such as a dragon. After each letter and item have been located, invite the class to chant about the letter and object. For example, have the class chant D *is for dragon, dragon, dragon.* D *is for dragon,* D, D, D!

Animalia

MATERIALS

reading window (see page 25)

Animalia by Graeme Base

Read *The Z Was Zapped* aloud. Invite children to guess the answer to the riddle presented on each page. Distribute a letter and a piece of construction paper to each child. Have children glue their letters to paper. Invite children to follow the pattern in the book and create an action for their letter, such as a boiling *B*, a flying *F*, or a jumping *J*. Have children decorate their letters to show the action. As children decorate, go around the room and write each child's idea on the back of his or her paper (e.g. *The J was jumping*). Collect papers and bind them into a class alphabet book.

The *B* Was Boiled

MATERIALS

The Z Was Zapped by Chris Van Allsburg

construction paper

die-cut uppercase letters (see page 24)

glue

crayons, markers

class book-binding materials and cover

Letter Raise

MATERIALS

nursery rhyme or poem
containing words beginning
with the same letter

chart paper

markers

tangible letters, all the same letter
(see page 24)

In advance, copy the nursery rhyme or poem on chart paper. Read the rhyme or poem to the class. Invite the class to repeat each line after you read it. Tell children the next time they hear the rhyme or poem they will become detectives and look for a special beginning letter. Distribute the letters. Ask children to place the letters on their hearts. Tell children that their hearts are "home position" for their letters. "Detectives" will prove they know the letter by placing it on their heads each time they hear and see it at the beginning of a word. Detectives should then place the letters back on their hearts. Read the rhyme or poem slowly, inviting children to place the letters on their heads when they hear appropriate words. Change the letter's destination, such as to the knee, and read the poem again—this time a little faster. As children become more proficient, change body positions and read the poem faster and faster until children break out in giggles and cannot keep up.

Alphabet in Disguise

MATERIALS

construction paper

die-cut upper- and lowercase
alphabets (see page 24)

glue

crayons, markers

class book-binding materials
and cover

Distribute a piece of construction paper and one die-cut letter to each child. Invite children to glue their letters, in any direction, on the paper. Invite each child to use crayons or markers to disguise his or her letter by turning it into an object or part of a scene. As children draw, go around the room and have each child complete the sentence, *I made a (object) from a (letter).* Copy the sentence on top of each child's paper. Collect papers and bind them into a class alphabet book.

I made an angel from an A.

Each morning, use an overhead projector and transparency to record and report the daily news. Invite three volunteers to tell you anything they would like to share. Paraphrase the information into one or two sentences and write them on the overhead as Daily News. In addition, add information you would like to share, such as news about field trips, birthdays, or meetings. Read aloud each sentence after it is written, and invite the class to repeat it after you. Read aloud and have children repeat the entire page when it is complete. Choose a letter-knowledge objective for the day, such as having children find letters they recognize, vowels, beginning letters of each word, or a specific letter. Invite volunteers to come to the overhead and place a rubber band around letters that meet the day's objective. On the transparency, tally the letters found. Invite children to count the tally marks when all letters have been found.

Daily News

MATERIALS

overhead projector, transparency, markers

rubber bands

In advance, write a short sentence on a sentence strip. Give each child a marker. Invite children to listen very closely while you say a sentence. Ask children to write down all the letters they hear. Distribute highlighting markers. Display the sentence, and invite children to highlight all the letters that are in both the sentence and on their papers.

Sentence Dictation

MATERIALS

sentence strip

markers

drawing paper

highlighting markers

Write the Room

MATERIALS

clipboards

pens

Letter Card reproducible
(page 125)

Choose six letters, write each one inside a small box on the Letter Card reproducible, and reproduce the filled-in chart for the class. Distribute Letter Card reproducibles, pens, and clipboards. Invite children to tour and "write the room," copying any word displayed in the classroom in the box that shows its first letter.

Lists

MATERIALS

chart paper

markers

Wikki-Stix (see page 24)

Have children brainstorm a list of items, such as animals with four legs, cartoon characters, or favorite places. Copy the list on chart paper. Invite children to come to the chart and use Wikki-Stix to underline special letters such as letters in their names, first letters, or letters you have identified by sound (such as /b/).

After reading aloud a favorite book, invite the class to use butcher paper, crayons, paint, and markers to make a mural showing a scene from the story. Have children name objects on the completed mural and say the beginning letter or sound of the object. Copy each object's name on an index card. Invite children to tape the cards next to the objects. After labeling the mural, ask volunteers to circle uppercase letters in blue marker and lowercase letters in green. Tally and orally count the number of upper- and lowercase letters.

Have children brainstorm items in the classroom. Make two labels for each item named. Ask children to help you label the room, taping labels at their eye level. Have children sort the second set of labels by first or last letters. On the board, record the first or last letters and tally how many words fit each category. Invite the class to read the letter names and count the tally marks.

MATERIALS

read-aloud picture book

butcher paper

crayons, markers

tempera paint, paintbrushes

index cards

tape

blue and green markers

Room Labels

MATERIALS

4" x 6" (10 cm x 15 cm) index cards

markers

tape

Letter Search

MATERIALS

3-M Post-it Tape Flags (see page 25)

Assign a letter to each child. (Choose a letter with which he or she has difficulty.) Have children become detectives and find their letters in the classroom—on word banks (see page 42), word walls (see page 42), bulletin boards, or labels. Have children place a tape flag over the letter each time he or she finds it. Continue the activity throughout the year as children's needs and room decorations change.

Animal Word Match

MATERIALS

farm animal pictures cut from magazines

index cards

glue

markers

pocket chart

card container

Farm Friends reproducible (page 126)

pencils

In advance, find and cut out farm animal pictures to match those on the Farm Friends reproducible. Glue each animal picture to an index card. Write the name of each animal on a separate index card. Display the animal words in a pocket chart in two columns to make a word wall. Place a container of picture cards below the chart. Invite a volunteer to choose a picture card. Have the volunteer say the animal's name three times. Have children guess the first letter in the animal's name. Invite the volunteer to find the word on the word wall and place the picture over the word so only the first letter shows. Say the first letter of the animal's name and then the animal's name, such as, *H, horse.* Invite children to record the first letter of the animal's name on the Farm Friends reproducible. For example, have children write *H* on top of the horse on the sheet. To continue the activity, place the materials in a learning center.

Choose five high-frequency words from a reading lesson that start with the same letter, such as *sale, saw, she, see,* and *said.* Have children read and recite the words several times. Copy and distribute Wand Words reproducibles. Have children make reading wands by making a loop in one end of a pipe cleaner and tying curling ribbon around the loop. Write the high-frequency words on the chalkboard. Have children copy each word on their recording sheet. Using a reading wand and a magazine, demonstrate how good readers scan a line of text from left to right to locate words in text. Invite children to use magazines, newspapers, old books, and their reading wands to scan and find words listed on their sheets. Have children cut out the words and place them in the correct boxes on their sheets.

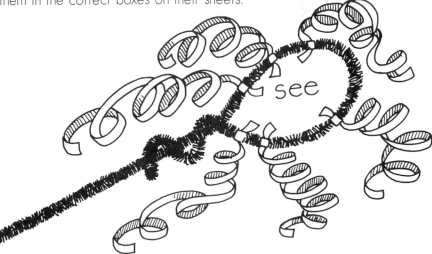

Display a word wall from a previous lesson. Invite children to use Cuisenaire rods to build five or more words from the word bank. Ask children to record the words they built and copy them three times to reinforce letter formation and visual memory.

Magazine Word Bank

MATERIALS

magazines, newspapers, old books

pipe cleaners

curling ribbon

Wand Words reproducible (page 127)

scissors

glue

Words with Rods

MATERIALS

word wall (see page 42)

Cuisenaire rods (see page 25)

writing paper

pencils

Environmental Print

MATERIALS

food box and can labels, newspaper and magazine advertisements

3" x 5" (7.5 cm x 12.5 cm) index cards

glue

name cards (see page 25)

tangible upper- and lowercase letters (see page 24)

drawing paper

pencils, crayons, markers

In advance, glue labels and advertisements to index cards. Laminate the cards. Have children use name cards as models and build their names with tangible letters. Under each letter, have children place an environmental-print card with a word that begins with the same letter. Have children write their names on drawing paper and draw the environmental-print picture or logo under each letter in their names. Invite children to repeat the activity with friends' names to make environmental print word banks.

ABC Wall

MATERIALS

butcher paper

markers

double-stick tape

rebus picture cards from recently-read books (see page 6)

card container

In advance, write the alphabet on a large piece of butcher paper. Laminate the butcher paper. Place a strip of double-stick tape beside each letter. Display the alphabet throughout the year. Invite children to sort the cards and place them on the alphabet wall next to each picture's beginning letter. Change picture cards frequently. Extension: Have children sort picture cards by their middle or ending letters.

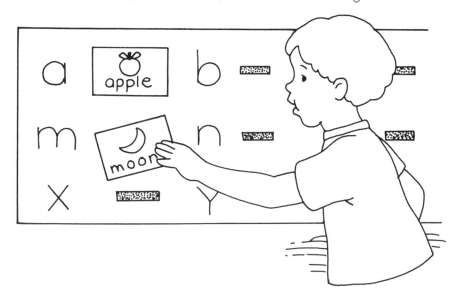

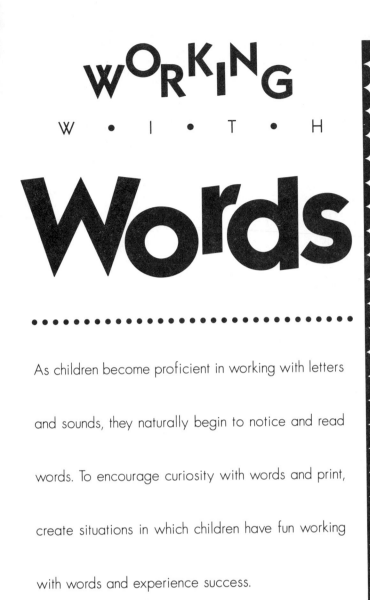

WORKING WITH Words

As children become proficient in working with letters and sounds, they naturally begin to notice and read words. To encourage curiosity with words and print, create situations in which children have fun working with words and experience success.

READING SKILLS

Working with words develops the following reading skills. Children who understand and can work with words:

- understand sentences are made up of separate words.
- know words have meaning, unlike letters and sounds.
- hear word sounds and can write the letters they represent.
- locate small words within larger words.
- sequence words to create meaning.
- locate words in text.
- use beginning and ending sounds as cues.
- scan words, attending to letters and word chunks to decode.
- recognize a word orally and its written match.

TEACHING STRATEGIES

The following teaching strategies offer unique ways to help children gain word knowledge. Pages 44 through 58 provide dozens of word activities. Each activity incorporates the use of reading manipulatives and one of these teaching strategies.

- Build words from letters and sounds, making words from smaller parts.
- Break down words into smaller words or letters and sounds.
- Use prior knowledge, context clues, and picture clues to develop sight-word vocabulary.
- Teach words through vocabulary games and literature-based activities.
- Develop word skills through spelling games, word comparisons, and writing.

READING MANIPULATIVES

Pages 42 and 43 show several reading manipulatives featured in this and other chapters. Consult these pages when making manipulatives, when deciding which manipulatives to use, and to determine possible substitutions.

Featured Reading Manipulatives

Carpet Squares

Many carpet stores will donate samples.

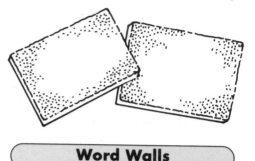

Word Walls

Create a large display of any group of words from units or lessons, recently-read books, brainstormed words, and sight or high-frequency words.

Pocket Word Banks

Write each letter of the alphabet on a library pocket. Display pockets on a bulletin board. Have children write correctly-spelled words on index cards and place them in the pockets for use at a later date.

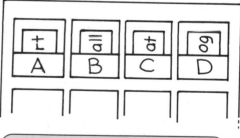

Large Number Line

Write each number on a section of bulletin-board border.

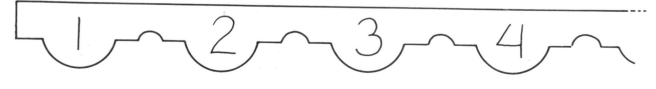

Popsicle-Stick Letters

Write upper- and lowercase letters on popsicle sticks with permanent marker.

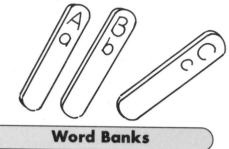

Word Banks

Have children generate personal word lists similar to personal dictionaries. They can be recorded in notebooks, file folders, or on the floor with tangible letters.

Word Patch

Cut a construction-paper patch. Attach two yarn pieces as ties. Tape the patch over words in text.

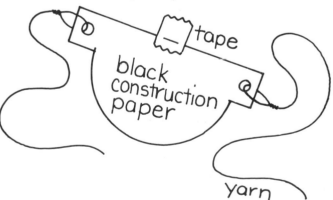

Featured Reading Manipulatives

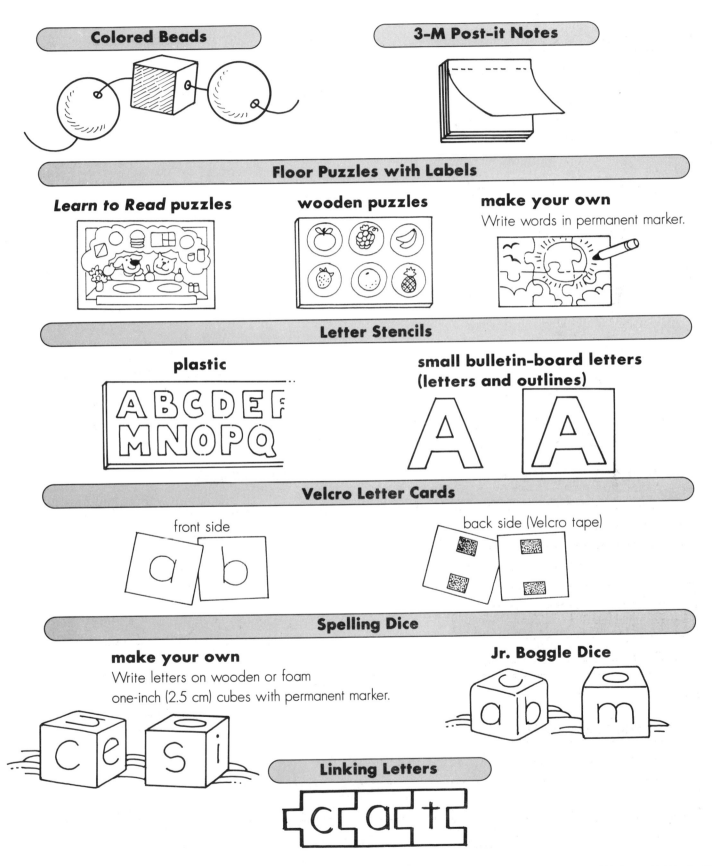

Colored Beads

3-M Post-it Notes

Floor Puzzles with Labels

Learn to Read puzzles

wooden puzzles

make your own
Write words in permanent marker.

Letter Stencils

plastic

small bulletin-board letters
(letters and outlines)

ABCDEF
MNOPQ

A   A

Velcro Letter Cards

front side

back side (Velcro tape)

a   b

Spelling Dice

make your own
Write letters on wooden or foam
one-inch (2.5 cm) cubes with permanent marker.

Jr. Boggle Dice

c   e   s   i

a   b   m

Linking Letters

c   a   t

Draw a Bug

MATERIALS

pocket word bank (see page 42)

magnetic letters (see page 24)

3" (7.5 cm) magnet strips

magnet board (see page 7)

Display a pocket word bank on or next to the chalkboard. Invite children to sequence magnetic letters at the top of a magnet board. Have a child (Player One) choose a word from the word bank. Ask Player One to place a three-inch magnet strip horizontally on the magnet board for each letter in the word he or she chose. For example, if Player One chooses the word *tree,* he or she lines up four magnet strips. Have other players take turns guessing letters that appear in the word. If a child correctly chooses a letter, he or she exchanges a magnetic letter for a magnet strip. (Player One tells him or her where to place the letter.) When a child guesses a letter *not* in the word, begin drawing an insect on the chalkboard. For each incorrect guess, draw an insect's head, thorax, abdomen, two antennae (one at a time), six legs (one at a time), and two eyes (one at a time). The object of the game is for players to guess the word before you draw a whole insect.

All Mixed Up

MATERIALS

rebus picture cards (see page 6)

card containers

tangible letters (see page 24)

word bank (see page 42)

In advance, place each picture card in a separate container. In the same container, place the tangible letters needed to spell the word. Demonstrate how to remove the picture card and letters and arrange the letters to spell the word. Say the word slowly. Ask yourself aloud, *What do I hear at the beginning of cat?* (Take the letter C and place it in front of you.) *What do I hear next?* (Take the letter A and place it in front of you.) *What do I hear at the end of cat?* (Take the letter T and place it in front of you.) Say the word. Give each child a container. Have children say picture names, build words, and then say them. (Since some children hear word endings first, invite children to place the letters out of order.) Have children trade containers until everyone has made all words. Invite children to record the words in their word banks.

In advance, spray-paint beans red and blue. Write the alphabet on the board, using pink chalk for vowels and blue chalk for consonants. Distribute a name card (not the child's own name), red and blue beans (at least five red and 21 blue), and a marker to each child. Invite children to use permanent marker to write a letter on each bean, writing vowels on red beans and consonants on blue. Have each child use the beans to build the name on his or her name card. (Invite children to borrow beans from friends if they need them.) Ask volunteers to tell the name they built, including the names of the vowels and consonants they used. Choose a vowel such as A. Invite the class to build a word with the letter A in it. Have each child read his or her word aloud and tell the name of the vowel and the other letters used. Have children record the words they build.

MATERIALS

large, dry, kidney-shaped beans

red and blue spray paint

pink and blue chalk

thin, black permanent markers

name cards (see page 25)

writing paper

One vowel. Two consonants.

In advance, use index cards and markers to write several words with the same vowel combination such as *igh*. *Igh* words could include *night*, *fight*, *sight*, *right*, *high*, and *sigh*. Distribute a set of tangible letters to each child. Have children place the letters in alphabetical order and take out the *i*, *g*, and *h*. Ask children to place the *igh* together in front of them. Explain that *igh* makes the long *I* sound, and demonstrate the sound. Tell children you are going to say several *igh* words. When you say a word, such as *night*, have children find the tangible letters needed to complete the word (*n* and *t*) and place them in front of and/or behind the *igh*. After each word is made, show the word card. Have children check their words, remove the letters, and get ready for the next word. Challenge children to build words as fast as they can. Have children record their two favorite words on writing paper.

Rearrange the *igh*

MATERIALS

tangible letters (see page 24)

index cards

markers

writing paper

pencils

abcdef jklmno

pq s uvwxyz

right

Popsicle-Stick Puzzle

MATERIALS

two sets of popsicle-stick letters (see page 42)

can

slates

chalk

Separate vowels from the letter sets. Place the consonants in a can. Divide children into pairs. Invite a child from each pair to close his or her eyes and choose five or six letters from the can. Ask pairs to use those letters and as many vowels as needed to make as many words as possible. Ask pairs to read aloud and record their words on slates after they make them. Play several rounds and invite children to choose new letters for each.

Word Builder

MATERIALS

sentence strips

markers

carpet squares (see page 42)

tangible letters (see page 24)

In advance, write several words on individual sentence strips. Draw bold lines between the letters to isolate separate sounds (not letters or syllables). For example, you would separate the word *truck* into three sections (tr/u/ck) and *coat* into three sections (c/oa/t). Choose a word from a sentence strip. Lay down carpet squares to show the number of sound sections in which the word is divided. For example, lay down three carpet squares for the word *coat*. Write the word on the chalkboard without the sound-separation lines. Ask a child to listen to and watch the word as you read it. Have the child use tangible letters to spell the word, and place each letter in the correct place on the squares. For example, the child would lay a *c* on the first square, *oa* on the second square, and *t* on the third. Reveal the sentence strip so the child can check his or her answer. Continue laying squares and having children build words until all strips are revealed. Extension: Have children jump from square to square as sounds are said.

Choose several words from a picture book that have all audible letters, and write each on a sentence strip. Read the book aloud and discuss it. Tell children they are going to play an echo game using words from the book. Divide the class into pairs and distribute several paper squares to each. Read aloud a sentence-strip word. Teach the class to echo, stretching out each sound in the word as if they are hearing an echo from a mountaintop. After you and the children echo back and forth several times, tell them how many letters/sounds are in the word. Invite each pair to use that number of paper squares to write the word, one letter on each square. Display the sentence strip so students can check and change their answers if necessary. To record, have children glue the correct letters on drawing paper to spell the word.

Writing Echoes

MATERIALS

read-aloud picture book

sentence strips

markers

small paper squares

pencils

drawing paper

glue

In advance, make a word wall or bank with large words containing smaller words, such as *dandelion, basketball, kitchen,* and *lightning.* Have children work with partners. Invite one partner to choose a word from the word wall and make it with tangible letters. Have partners read the long word aloud together. Invite the other partner to break up the word, separating letters to isolate the smaller word inside. Have partners read the small word aloud. Invite partners to change positions and play the game until they have made and broken up each word.

Make and Break

MATERIALS

tangible letters (see page 24)

word wall or bank (see page 42)

writing paper

pencils

Little Word Look

MATERIALS

sentence strips

markers

pocket chart

two craft sticks

In advance, write several big words that contain little words on sentence strips. Words could include *gingerbread, history, butterfly,* and *cargo.* (Be sure you can *hear* little words within big words and not just see them. For example, for the little word *in,* use *window* rather than *king.*) Place words inside a pocket chart. Read each word aloud slowly. Invite children to read the words after you read them and then read the words aloud with you. Call a volunteer to the chart. Invite the volunteer to read the first big word and use the craft sticks to frame the little word inside. If there are two little words in a big word, have the volunteer frame the second word as well. Continue calling volunteers until every word has been framed.

Word/Number Books

MATERIALS

sentence strips

pocket chart

markers

ten-page blank books

word wall or bank (see page 42)

pencils, crayons, markers

alphabet pasta (see page 24)

glue

In advance, write ten unfinished sentences on sentence strips. The first sentence should read: _____ *is a word with* _____ *letter.* The other nine sentences should read: _____ *is a word with* _____ *letters.* Place sentences vertically in the pocket chart. Number the sentences one through ten. Distribute a blank book and approximately 55 pieces of alphabet pasta to each child. Have children consult a word wall or bank to find a word with one letter. Ask children to copy the first sentence from the pocket chart on page one of their books. Children should start the sentence with the one-letter word they found and fill the second blank by gluing one pasta letter in the space. [For example, A *is a word with* (one piece of A *pasta*) *letter.*] Have children repeat the activity with sentences two through ten by finding two- through ten-letter words and gluing on the appropriate number of pasta pieces. After each page is complete and dried, invite children to decorate their pages.

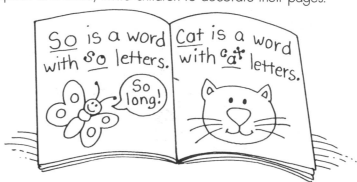

In advance, write each sentence from the emergent reader on a sentence strip. Tape the large number line to the floor. Read the emergent reader aloud. After reading, display and read each sentence strip. Cut apart each word in the sentences. Challenge children to use the number line and place each word under the number that shows how many letters it has. For example, the word *noisy* would be placed under number 5. Invite volunteers to use letter clues to read each word. Have children copy words from a column that has at least three words.

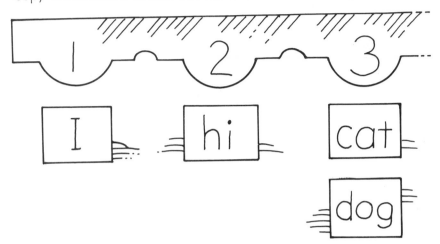

In advance, determine the number of words and squares to be used in the game (nine or sixteen, see reproducible). Reproduce and cut out Word Bingo cards with the chosen number of squares. Distribute counters and Bingo cards. Choose a child to call words. To prepare for the game, have children read aloud words from a word wall or bank and write a word in any square on their cards. (Children should write words randomly, not in order.) To play, have the caller call words in random order and write each word on a list after he or she says it. When children find the word on their cards, have them cover it with a counter. When a player covers a row horizontally, diagonally, or vertically, he or she should call out, *Winning words!* If all of his or her words were called, he or she becomes the new caller and play begins again.

Shortest to Longest

MATERIALS

emergent reader

sentence strips

markers

scissors

large number line (see page 42)

writing paper

pencils

Word Bingo

MATERIALS

Word Bingo reproducible (page 128)

word wall or bank (see page 42)

counters (see page 24)

I Spy with My Little Eye

MATERIALS

big book

word patch (see page 42)

tape

Read aloud a favorite big book. After reading, choose a word on the page that is shown in the picture, and tape a word patch over it. (Do not show children the page or word as it is being covered.) Display the page. Give clues for the word's identity, beginning with, *I spy with my little eye.* (For example, *I spy with my little eye something white, with long ears, and begins with the letter* R.) Have children survey the page to find the word's identity. Uncover the word and invite children to read it aloud. Continue covering with the word patch and giving clues for several words.

I See Colors

MATERIALS

I See Colors by Rozanne Lanczak Williams

I See Colors reproducible (page 129)

colored beads (see page 43)

Read aloud *I See Colors.* Distribute a reproducible to each child. Explain the color key at the top of the page, inviting children to place a green bead next to the word *I,* a red bead next to the word *see,* and a blue bead next to the word *colors.* Ask children to read the reproducible and place a bead under each word. (Children will place green beads under the *I's,* red beads under the *see's,* and blue beads under the color words.) Invite children to read the sentences aloud after placing the beads. Place the book and beads in a learning center. Invite children to complete the activity independently with the book.

Complete the Daily News activity as described on page 35. Instead of having volunteers circle known letters with rubber bands, have them circle words they recognize. Invite children to trace one of their hands on drawing paper and write a recognized word from the daily news on each finger. Invite each child to read the words he or she recognizes.

(see page 35)

as described on page 35

Handy Words

MATERIALS

Daily News activity (see page 35)

rubber bands

drawing paper

pencils

In advance, choose a current topic of study, such as animals, from which to create a web. Using yarn, make a large circle on the floor. Use tangible letters to build the topic word (animals) in the center of the circle. Choose four general categories that pertain to the word, such as *farm animals, jungle animals, water animals,* and *desert animals,* and write each on an index card. Extend yarn strings from the top, bottom, and sides of the circle, placing an index card at the end of each. Explain the word web, telling students they will build words to show what they know about the topic in the web's center. Divide the class into four groups, and send each group to a different yarn string/category card. Give each group tangible letters. Ask children to use the letters to build words in their category. Have children build their words on each side of their category's yarn string. When the web is finished, invite each group to read their words. Congratulate the class on knowing so much about the web's topic. Record the web to make a word-wall writing resource.

Word Web

MATERIALS

tangible letters (see page 24)

index cards

markers

four yarn skeins

scissors

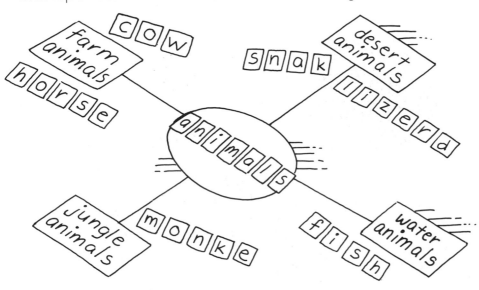

Puzzling Words

MATERIALS

Learn to Read floor puzzle or any puzzle with labels (see page 43)

index cards

markers

counters (see page 24)

In advance, write each word from the puzzle on index cards. Have a group of children build the puzzle. Place the word cards face down in a pile next to the puzzle. Distribute several counters to each child. Have a child choose a word from the pile. Invite the child to find the matching word on the puzzle and use puzzle picture clues to read the word aloud. If the child succeeds, invite him or her to place a counter on that word in the puzzle. If the child cannot read the word, point to the picture. Invite children to take turns matching and reading words.

Word Treasure Chest

MATERIALS

empty baby-wipe boxes

plastic jewels, sequins, or glitter

glue

index cards

several emergent readers and read-aloud favorites

letter stencils (see page 43)

pencils, pens

In advance, have each child make a word treasure chest by gluing plastic jewels, sequins, or glitter to an empty baby-wipe box. Each time you read a story aloud, choose two or three children to add some treasures (words) to their word treasure chests. Invite the class to use stencils and trace a sight word from the story. Ask volunteers to show and read their words to the class. Have children place the cards in their treasure chests. Invite children to practice reading their treasures whenever they wish. Each week, choose children to add to the treasure. Encourage each child to read his or her treasure at least once a week to review old words and practice new ones that have been added. Once a month, invite children to read words to you. If you wish, keep a record of words missed and mastered. At the end of the month, clean out the treasure chests and start over with new words.

In advance, choose three word categories with which you want children to work, such as color words, animal words, and three-letter words. Be sure word categories appear in the chosen big book. Write an example of each word on tagboard. (For example, *red*—color word, *horse*—animal word, and *bag*—three-letter word.) Use a red, blue, or green marker for each word. Read aloud a favorite big book. Display and explain each word category. Invite volunteers to mark words that fit into each category with red, blue, and green tape flags. After children flag the words, read the book aloud again and check their work, searching for missed words and congratulating correct answers.

Word Find

MATERIALS

big book

tagboard

red, blue, and green markers

red, blue, and green 3-M Post-it Tape Flags (see page 25)

In advance, copy each word from "Humpty Dumpty" on individual index cards. Place the word cards in a pocket chart. Teach "Humpty Dumpty" orally without the pocket chart or pictures. Enlarge, copy, and distribute the reproducible. Have children cut out the pictures and place them in order to build the nursery rhyme. Display the pocket chart and remove a word card. (Place the card face up in front of you.) Read the nursery rhyme aloud until you come to the missing word. Invite a volunteer to place a picture card in the missing word's place. Repeat the activity with several words and pictures until the whole rhyme is replaced with pictures. (Place the removed word cards in front of you, out of order.) Reverse the activity and have children replace picture cards with word cards.

Rhyme Time

MATERIALS

index cards

markers

pocket chart

Humpty Dumpty reproducible (page 130)

scissors

Pipe-Cleaner Pyramid

▼▼▼▼▼▼▼▼

MATERIALS

read-aloud picture book

pipe cleaners

index cards

markers

Place a large, eight-layer pyramid of pipe cleaners on the floor. On index cards, write numbers one through eight and place each next to a pyramid layer. Read the book aloud. Have children gather around the pyramid. Tell children that a word will go above each pipe cleaner, and there are rules for each line of the pipe-cleaner pyramid. For line one, have children name the story's main character. Write it on an index card and place it above the top pipe cleaner. For line two, have children name two words to describe the character. Write the words on cards and place them on line two. For line three, have children think of three words to describe the setting. For line four, have students think of four words that state the story's problem or plot. For line five, ask students to think of five words that describe a main event. For line six, have students think of six words explaining the climax. For line seven, have students think of seven words that tell the story's solution. For line eight, have students think of eight words that tell the ending. Invite children to read the pyramid back to you.

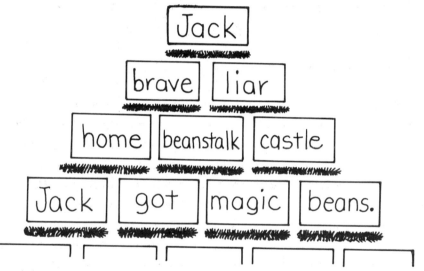

Mini Post-it Notebooks

▼▼▼▼▼▼▼▼

MATERIALS

emergent reader featuring a specific vowel sound

small 3-M Post-it Notes (see page 43)

stapler

pencils

Read the emergent reader aloud. Distribute several Post-it Notes to each child. Read the story again, inviting children to find words that contain a specific vowel sound, such as *bed, dent,* and *bench.* Each time children hear and see a word with the sound, have them raise their hands to identify it. Ask a volunteer to point out the word. Ask children to copy the word on a Post-it Note. Continue the activity through the rest of the story. Invite children to staple their Post-it Notes together to make a mini-book. Ask children to read their mini-books each day for a week. At the end of the week, invite children to read their books to you.

In advance, write each word of a favorite nursery rhyme on separate index cards. Place the cards, in order, in the pocket chart. Teach the nursery rhyme by reading it aloud, having children read each line after you read it, and by reading it together. Ask children to close their eyes. Choose a helper. For each line of the rhyme, have the helper turn over one word card so it cannot been seen. Have children open their eyes. Invite children to reread the rhyme aloud while the helper points to each word. Have students whisper the missing word as the helper points to the turned-over card. Invite new helpers to turn over and point to words until all words are hidden and children can whisper the entire rhyme.

No Peeking!

MATERIALS

nursery rhyme

index cards

markers

pocket chart

Play this game to introduce new reading vocabulary. In advance, write vocabulary words from the emergent reader on index cards. Take children outside and line them up on the blacktop or sidewalk. Invite a child to choose a card and write the word, in very large letters, in sidewalk chalk. As the child is writing, have the class repeat the word after you and give examples of how the word might be used in a sentence. Have the first two or three children roll and guide the hula hoop over the letters in the word. Ask each child to say the word as he or she begins rolling, and say it again as he or she finishes rolling. Repeat the activity with each word card, going down the line and inviting two or three children to roll. Variation: Have children jump, hop, or stomp along the letters.

Rolling Along

MATERIALS

emergent reader

index cards

markers

sidewalk chalk

hula hoops

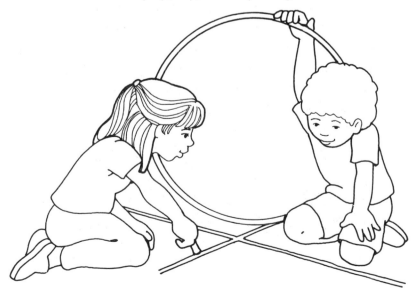

Word Pairs

MATERIALS

Word Pairs reproducible (page 131) or word pairs from an emergent reader

scissors

two index cards

markers

pocket chart

colored tape

slates

chalk

In advance, reproduce the word pairs and cut them apart. Label two index cards *same* and *different*. Divide a pocket chart in half with colored tape and place the *same* label on the top left and the *different* label on the top right. Have children sort word pairs by placing words that are the same in the *same* column and words that are different in the *different* column. To help students check their work, read the words aloud after sorting. Invite children to rearrange word pairs if there are mistakes. Invite children to record words from the *same* column on slates.

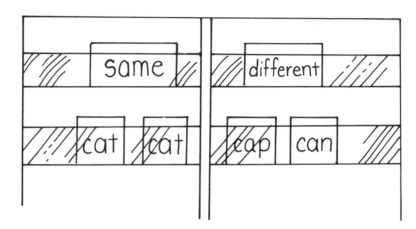

Word Fence

MATERIALS

ten index cards

markers

Velcro tape

Velcro letter cards (see page 43)

card containers

slates

chalk

In advance, write the words *hat, pig, bug, hill, cot, jump, cap,* and *pet* on individual index cards (or use words with short vowel sounds from an emergent reader). Laminate the cards. Place a small piece of Velcro tape under the first letter of each word. Display and read the word cards. Divide the class into pairs. Give a word and a set of letter cards to each pair. Have the pairs "velcro" each letter card to the beginning of their word to see if they can make new words. (For example, students might make the words *bat, cat, fat, mat, pat, rat, sat, tat,* and *vat* from the word *hat.*) Have children record their findings on slates. Invite pairs to share their words with the class.

Read aloud *The Cat in the Hat*. Invite children to listen for words with the same ending sound. Make a list of rhyming words on chart paper. If you wish, sketch a picture for each word. Invite children to make rhyming word pairs with Linking Letters.

Photocopy and distribute the "Are You Sleeping?" reproducible. Teach children to sing the original song. Tell children they will help you change the song and learn to spell three-letter words at the same time. Generate a list of three-letter words from a picture book. Circle two or three words for the class to spell and read. Using the bottom of the reproducible as a model, create a new song with the new three-letter words. Write the new song on sentence strips and place them in the pocket chart. Have the class sing the new song. Extension: Use other tunes to create songs for four-, five-, and six-letter words.

Cat—Hat

MATERIALS

The Cat in the Hat by Dr. Seuss or any rhyming picture book

chart paper

markers

Linking Letters (see page 43)

Spelling with Songs

MATERIALS

"Are You Sleeping?" reproducible (page 132)

picture book

sentence strips

markers

pocket chart

Spelling Dice

MATERIALS

spelling dice (see page 43)

Color Word Cards reproducible (page 133)

tangible letters (see page 24)

In advance, make two spelling dice and reproduce and cut out a color card for each child. Divide children into groups of six. Distribute a color card to each child, and place a set of tangible letters in the center of each group. Invite the first player to roll the spelling dice. If the dice show any letters found on the player's word card, have the player place tangible letters over the letters on the card. Have children take turns rolling and covering letters until one player covers his or her word. Have children trade cards and play again.

Make a Word

MATERIALS

five letter-tile alphabets (see page 24)

paper lunch bags

writing paper

pencils

In advance, set aside vowels from five sets of letter tiles. Place each set of consonant letter tiles in one of five paper bags. Play this game with five children. To model, invite a volunteer to reach in a paper bag and choose five or six consonant tiles. Help the volunteer make as many words as possible using the consonants he or she chose and the set-aside vowels. Ask the volunteer to record each word on paper. Distribute a bag, vowel set, and paper to each child. To play, have children choose tiles, make words, and record them. When children cannot make any more words, have them place the tiles back in the bag and choose new ones.

WORKING
W • I • T • H
Sentences

When children work with sentences, they accomplish several important tasks. They build vocabulary that will be used over and over again, reinforce letter and sound knowledge, and prepare themselves to read entire paragraphs and books.

READING SKILLS

Working with sentences develops the following reading skills. Children who understand and can work with sentences:

- understand sentences are made up of words.
- know sentences express whole ideas.
- place words in order so they make sense.
- understand punctuation and can punctuate correctly.
- use context clues to learn new words.
- link known words to unknown words.
- self-check and self-correct when reading a sentence.
- use meaning and sentence structure as cues.
- cross-check cue sources, comparing syntax, semantics, and graphophonics to figure out words and make meaning.

TEACHING STRATEGIES

The following teaching strategies offer unique ways to help children gain sentence knowledge. Pages 62 through 76 provide dozens of sentence activities. Each activity incorporates the use of reading manipulatives and one of these teaching strategies.

- Build sentences from individual words.
- Use hands-on punctuation demonstrations and sorting games.
- Have children experience hide-and-seek activities, guessing games, and dramatic play.
- Break sentences into parts to develop comprehension and the understanding of sentence structure.
- Use reading-strategy games and literature-based activities to develop self-monitoring skills.

READING MANIPULATIVES

Pages 60 and 61 show several reading manipulatives featured in this and other chapters. Consult these pages when making manipulatives, when deciding which manipulatives to use, and to determine possible substitutions.

Featured Reading Manipulatives

Sponge Letters

Available at craft supply stores.

Sentence Cubes

Write a word on each side of closed, medium-sized boxes in permanent marker.

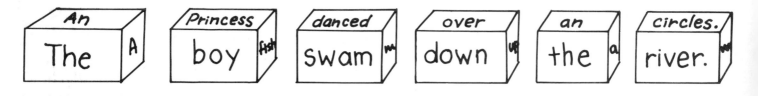

Bowling Sets

purchased plastic or cloth toys   **make your own**

Sandwich-Board Punctuation Marks

Attach two pieces of tagboard with yarn shoulder straps. Write desired information in permanent marker.

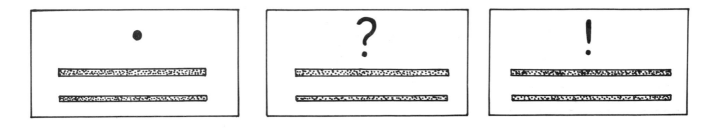

Featured Reading Manipulatives

Featured Reading Manipulatives

Sorting Walls

Use butcher paper and Velcro tape.

Word Slides

Fold the top and bottom edges of a piece of rectangular tagboard.

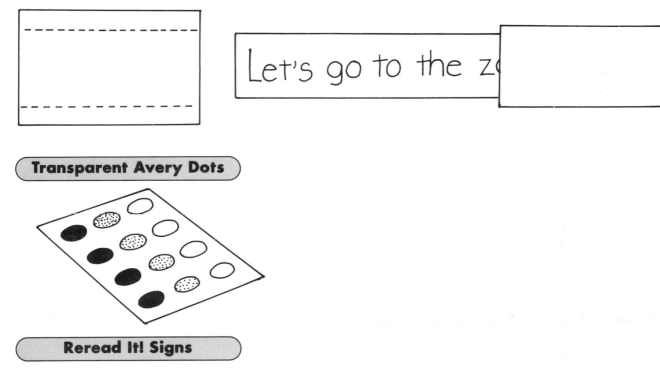

Let's go to the z○

Transparent Avery Dots

Reread It! Signs

Tape construction-paper circles to craft sticks. Write on signs with crayons or markers.

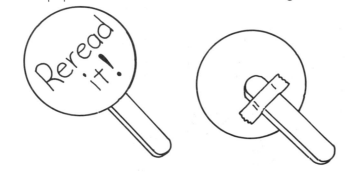

Speech Bubbles

MATERIALS

transparency of cartoon with one-sentence speech bubble

overhead projector

jump ropes

tangible letters (see page 24)

Wikki-Stix (see page 24)

On the overhead, display and read the cartoon. Explain the cartoon and the purpose of the speech bubble. Have children work in pairs. Have each pair lay a jump rope in a circle with a pointed end like a speech bubble. Invite pairs to think of one important thing they want to tell you. Have children use tangible letters to build the sentence inside the bubble. Ask children to place a Wikki-Stix between each word so you know where each word starts and ends. Walk around the room, offering help to those who need it. Invite each pair to read their sentence. Respond to each speech-bubble message.

Sponge Sentences

MATERIALS

read-aloud picture book with changeable ending

paper slips

butcher paper

crayons, markers

sponge letters (see page 60)

tempera paint

Give a slip of paper and a large piece of butcher paper to each child. Read aloud the picture book. Ask each child to think about how he or she could change the story's ending. Have children use crayons and markers to illustrate the new ending to the story on butcher paper. While children are drawing, ask each child to tell you a sentence that explains his or her new ending. Write the sentence on a slip of paper. Distribute sponge letters and paint. Have children copy the sentence by sponge-painting it at the bottom of their pictures. After pictures have dried, bind them into a class book entitled *A New Ending for (book title)*.

In advance, make several sentence cubes. Be sure cubes include words from all parts of speech and ending punctuation so sentences can be made. Work with a small group. Read aloud all words from the sentence cubes. Invite the group to line up the cubes to make a sentence and then read it aloud. Invite the group to rearrange the boxes until they have made and read several sentences. Make other sentence cubes based on favorite stories.

Sentence Cubes

MATERIALS

sentence cubes (see page 60)

In advance, write a three-sentence letter to the class. (Be sure the letter relates to a current topic of study or classroom event.) Write each word on an index card. Place the date, *Dear Class,* and *Sincerely,* in the pocket chart. Place the other word cards, out of order, on the floor. Tell children you have written a letter for them to build with word cards by following clues. For the first clue, tell children how many words are in the first sentence. Invite a volunteer to look at the words and guess the sentence. Remind children that the first word begins with a capital letter. (Most likely, children will not guess correctly with one clue.) For the second clue, tell children the first letter of the first or second word. Give clues for sentence one until the sentence is built. As children guess the correct words, invite them to place the words in the pocket chart. Continue giving clues for each sentence. After the letter is built, read it aloud. Have the class count and tell how many sentences are in the letter and how many words are in each sentence.

Build a Letter

MATERIALS

pocket chart

index cards

markers

Sentence Bowling

~~~~~~~~~~~~

MATERIALS

two bowling sets (see page 60)

Bowling Score Sheet reproducible (page 134)

Play this game with the help of a teacher's aide or other helper. Reproduce a score sheet for each child. Divide the class in half, sending each half to a different bowling set. Stay at one set to keep score while your helper keeps score at the other set. Invite each child to bowl. (Show children how to set up pins for the next person.) Have children count the number of pins they knock down during a turn. Challenge each child to make up a sentence with that number of words. For example, if a child knocks down four pins, he or she might say, *I eat green beans.* Invite children to call on friends for help, if needed. To keep score, write each child's sentence on his or her score sheet next to *Frame 1.* Invite each child to take three turns, recording each sentence. To close, have children count the words on their score sheet to determine their scores.

Shake, Take, and Make

~~~~~~~~~~~~

MATERIALS

several sets of three cans

popsicle sticks

thin marker

old business cards

pencils

In advance, use a thin marker to write words on popsicle sticks. Write at least ten words (or word groups) in each of three categories: names of people or animals such as *Jeffrey* or *Leo the Lion*, places such as *the candy store*, and past-tense actions such as *baked* or *danced*. Place each category in three separate cans labeled *Who?*, *Where?*, and *What?* Make one set for every two children. Have children work in pairs. Distribute a set of cans, several old business cards, and a pencil to each pair. Invite children to shake each can and remove a popsicle stick from each. Have children use the chosen sticks to make a sentence. Children can fill in missing words from the sentence by writing them on business cards. Invite each pair to read aloud the sentence they made. Have children shake, take, and make several sentences.

Punched-Out Punctuation

Using individual sentence strips, copy sentences from the emergent reader that use the same punctuation mark. Make one sentence for each child. Read the emergent reader aloud twice. The second time through, point out the featured punctuation mark each time it appears. Distribute sentence strips. Invite each child to read his or her sentence aloud. Invite children to use a hole puncher to punch out their punctuation mark, leaving a hole, or holes, in the sentence strip. Give a blank sentence strip, pencil, and glue to each child. Ask children to write a sentence with the same punctuation mark they punched out. Have children glue the punched-out dots from the first sentence strip on their new sentences to make the necessary punctuation marks. Invite each child to read his or her sentence.

MATERIALS

emergent reader

sentence strips

markers

hole punchers

pencils

glue

Dictation

In advance, use words from the Sentence Makers reproducible to write several dictation sentences on sentence strips. Copy and distribute the reproducible, along with scissors, construction paper, and glue. Have children cut the Sentence Makers apart and place them in random order. Dictate the first sentence from a sentence strip, and repeat it several times. Invite children to listen carefully to the words, find them in their Sentence Makers, and place them on construction paper to make the dictated sentence. Reveal the sentence strip. Have children rearrange words, if necessary, and glue them to the paper. Continue the activity with the remaining sentence strips. For subsequent lessons, use sentences from favorite emergent readers.

MATERIALS

Sentence Makers reproducible (page 135)

sentence strips

markers

scissors

construction paper

glue

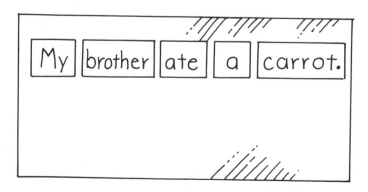

Commas

Make a sentence strip for each child. Each sentence should come from the emergent reader and include commas. Do not write the commas in the sentences. Read the emergent reader aloud twice. The second time, point out commas each time they appear. Explain that commas are used to separate words in a list so we pause when we read the words. Distribute a sentence strip, macaroni, and glue to each child. Have children read their sentences and decide where to glue macaroni "commas." Invite children to read their sentences aloud and pause when they come to macaroni commas.

He ran over, under, and through it.

Will the Real Punctuation Mark Please Stand Up?

Using individual sentence strips, copy several emergent-reader sentences that use different ending punctuation marks. Cover the marks with tape. Read the emergent reader aloud twice. The second time through, point out punctuation marks. Display the first sentence strip and read it aloud. Choose three children to put on punctuation sandwich boards. Display the sentence strip. Ask the child wearing the period to stand at the end of the sentence. Invite the class to read the sentence aloud as a statement. Have the child wearing the period sit down. Ask the question-mark child to stand at the end of the sentence. Invite the class to read the sentence aloud as a question. Repeat the activity with the child wearing the exclamation point, having children read the sentence as an exclamation. Invite children to guess which punctuation mark is correct for the sentence. Ask, *Will the real punctuation mark please stand up?* Have the child wearing the correct punctuation mark stand. Uncover the mark and have the class read the sentence with the correct inflection. Choose new children to be punctuation marks and repeat the activity with each sentence.

Do you know my sister☐

In advance, write several dialogue sentences (minus the quotation marks) from a big book on individual sentence strips. Place each sentence in a pocket chart. Use red marker to draw a quotation mark on each of four clothespins. Read aloud the big book twice, drawing attention to the quotation marks during the second reading. Explain that quotation marks are like open lips—the words a character says are inside them. Display the pocket chart. Read the first sentence aloud, using expression during the dialogue. Invite a child to come up and clip the quotation marks (the four clothespins) on the chart around the spoken words. Have the child explain why he or she placed the clothespins in those positions. Help the child move the clothespins if he or she made an error. Ask the child to read the sentence with expression. Invite volunteers to clip the marks on each sentence, explain their placement, and read the sentences aloud.

In advance, post three sorting walls. At the top of each wall, draw a period, question mark, or exclamation point. Discuss a current topic of study. Write children's questions, comments, and exclamations on sentence strips using correct punctuation. Place Velcro tape on the back of each sentence. Display the sentences on the floor and read them aloud with expression. Explain the punctuation marks on the sorting walls. Invite children to sort the sentences by punctuation mark and attach them to the correct wall. Divide the class into three groups, and have each group read a wall. For older children, cover the punctuation marks with colored tape, and invite children to sort the sentences by reading the words for meaning. After sorting, have children uncover each punctuation mark to reveal the correct answers.

Clip the Lips

MATERIALS

big book featuring dialogue and quotation marks

pocket chart

sentence strips

black and red markers

clothespins

Sort the Sentences

MATERIALS

three sorting walls (see page 61)

overhead pens

sentence strips

markers

Velcro tape

colored tape

Story Problems

MATERIALS

counters (see page 24)

overhead projector, transparency, markers

drawing paper

crayons, pencils

In advance, think of an easily-visualized story problem such as *Three horses ran into the field. Two horses came up and joined the three. How many horses are in the field?* Write the problem on the overhead projector. Take children through a four-step process that makes story problems easy and helps them write one-sentence answers. Read the story problem aloud to the class. First, invite volunteers to act out the problem. Second, have children make the problem with counters. Third, ask children for a one-sentence answer such as *Five horses are in the field.* Write the answer on the board. Have children draw and decorate the problem on drawing paper, copying the answer below their pictures.

What Sounds Right?

MATERIALS

big book

old business cards

markers

masking tape

In advance, choose a word from the first page of the big book and copy it on a business card. Write two other words for the chosen word that would not make sense in the sentence. For example, if the sentence was *Who eats berries?*, you might write the words *berries, very,* and *went* on business cards. Place a piece of tape on each card. Stack the cards in random order and tape the set to the word in the book. Repeat the process for each book page. Explain that the book has a problem—there are words in it that don't belong. Tell children they will be detectives and try to figure out which word sounds right for each sentence. Read the first sentence aloud three times. The first time, read it with the top card. Remove the top card. The second time, read the sentence with the second card. Remove that card. Read the sentence with the third card. Do *not* remove the third card. Have children consider the three words and decide which word makes sense in the sentence. Remove the last card and reveal the text so children can check their predictions.

In advance, make a word slide for each child. Using sentence strips and markers, write two sentences from a picture book for each child. Write two additional sentences for demonstration. Read aloud and discuss the picture book. Using one demonstration sentence, model the activity. First, hide the sentence from the class and place a word slide over a word you want to hide. Show the sentence strip. Read the sentence aloud, skipping the covered word. Slowly reveal the word by sliding the word slide and uncovering the first letter. Invite volunteers to guess the missing word. If no one guesses the word, remind them of the story and reread the sentence, uncovering the second letter. Again, ask volunteers to guess the word. When the word is guessed, take off the word slide and have everyone read the sentence aloud. Model the activity with the second demonstration sentence. Divide the class into pairs. Distribute two sentences and a word slide to each pair. Invite partners to take turns hiding and guessing words.

MATERIALS

read-aloud picture book

word slides (see page 61)

sentence strips

markers

Families share the hard

In advance, write a silly sentence for each child. (Sentence ideas can be taken from a unit of study or a favorite picture book.) Sentences should include a word or group of words at the end that makes that sentence's information incorrect, such as *A car flies*, or *A doctor works in the grocery store*. Distribute a sentence and scissors to each child. Have children read their sentences aloud. Ask children to find the incorrect words at the end of their sentences and cut them off. Distribute butcher paper, alphabet pretzels, and glue. Have children glue their sentence strips to paper. Using alphabet pretzels and glue, have children add new words to the ends of their sentences so they make sense. Invite children to illustrate their sentences.

Find the Mistakes

MATERIALS

sentence strips

scissors

butcher paper

alphabet pretzels (see page 24)

glue

markers, crayons

A car goes down the road.

A car flies.

Watermelon Hunt

MATERIALS

transparent Avery Dots (see page 61)

large watermelon

Watermelon Clues reproducible (page 136)

markers

knife

paper plates

napkins

In advance, write numbers one through ten on individual Avery Dots. Place the dots in plain view around the classroom or playground, adhering them to various objects. Reproduce and cut apart the Watermelon Clues, hiding each near its corresponding Avery Dot. Hide the watermelon near sentence ten. Tell the class they are going on a treasure hunt for a special object. Explain that clues to the object's identity are hidden near numbered dots. Have the class find dot number one and locate the first clue. Ask a volunteer to read the clue aloud. Have children guess the identity of the special object. Have the class continue to search for clues two through ten, read them, and guess the object after reading each clue. (If children find clues out of order, leave them in their place until it is "their turn" to be found and read.) When students find the watermelon, cut it open and enjoy! For other lessons, write new clues and hunt for a pumpkin or new classroom library book.

What's Missing?

MATERIALS

identical emergent readers and companion big book

colored tape

In advance, prepare an emergent reader for every two children. Using colored tape, cover the same key words in each sentence of all the books. Cover the same words in the big book. Explain that one way to figure out a word is to read the words around it. Divide the class into pairs. Distribute an emergent reader to each pair. Together, read the books aloud, using the big book to model. After reading a page, have children reread the first sentence. Invite each child to tell his or her partner a prediction for the words under the tape. As a class, count to three. On three, have children remove the tape from the sentence to check their predictions. Repeat the activity with each sentence. Use the same strategy with big books throughout the year.

In advance, copy each sentence, word by word, from an eight-page emergent reader on separate index cards. Place sentences on the floor, leaving two to three feet between each one. Mix up the words in each sentence. Place a copy of the emergent reader, open to the page that features each sentence, under each set of index cards. Explain that we always read from left to right. Read the emergent reader aloud, sweeping your finger or a pointer along the words. During the second read, invite a child to sweep his or her finger from left to right as you and the class read aloud. Explain that you have a friend who always reads out of order and needs help reading from left to right. Divide children into groups. Send each group to a different sentence. Challenge groups to arrange their sentences from left to right, checking their work with the emergent reader. After each group has rearranged their sentence, have them read their sentence aloud, walking from left to right along the words as they read them.

Order It

MATERIALS

several identical emergent readers

index cards

markers

Using sentence strips, write sentences from an emergent reader that describes a character performing an action, such as *The gingerbread man ran away.* Write a sentence for each child. Read aloud the emergent reader two times. During the second read, invite volunteers to point out sentences that describe a character performing an action. Distribute a puppet and sentence to each child. Have children sit on the floor in a circle. Invite each child to read his or her sentence aloud and make the puppet perform the action in the sentence.

Find the Action

MATERIALS

emergent reader

sentence strips

markers

puppets (see page 7)

The gingerbread man ran a[way]

Person, Place, or Thing?

~~~~~~~~

MATERIALS

three carpet squares

three index cards

markers

rebus picture cards (see page 6)

sentence strips

tape

In advance, write several sentences on sentence strips, taping rebus picture cards in place of nouns. For example, use *horse* and *barn* rebus picture cards to make the sentence *The horse is in the barn*. Lay out and label (with index cards) three carpet squares. Label one square *person*, one *place*, and the last *thing*. Discuss the word *noun* and its meaning. Give examples of people, places, and things. Display a sentence strip. Read the sentence strip aloud. Tell children the picture cards represent nouns. Show children how to remove the pictures from the sentences and sort them by laying them on the correct carpet square. For example, lay the *horse* picture card on the *thing* carpet square. Display remaining sentences. Invite children to read the sentences aloud and sort the nouns on carpet squares. After all cards are sorted, "read" each carpet square and have children make any necessary changes.

Take One Away

~~~~~~~~

MATERIALS

poem with complete sentences

pocket chart

index cards

markers

butcher paper

paint, paintbrushes

Write each word from the poem on separate index cards. Place the poem in the pocket chart, using one pocket for each sentence. Read the poem aloud two times, inviting children to read with you the second time. Have a child remove and read one word from the poem. Invite another child to offer a replacement for the word so the sentence still makes sense. For example, if the original sentence said, *I always like summer best,* a child may suggest to replace the word *summer* with *swimming* or the word *best* for *least*. Write the new word on an index card and place it in the chart over the old word. Continue with each sentence until a new poem is made. Have the class read the new poem aloud. Copy the poem on a piece of butcher paper and invite the class to paint a scene about their new poem.

In advance, write each sentence of the nursery rhyme on sentence strips, and place them in the pocket chart. Write the words *noun, verb,* and *other word* in a vertical list on chart paper. Place a blue dot next to *noun,* a green dot next to *verb,* and a red dot next to *other word.* Post the chart next to the pocket chart. Read the nursery rhyme aloud. Read aloud and explain the color/dot chart. Explain the meaning of the words *noun* and *verb.* Challenge children to place a dot on each word to show if it is a noun, verb, or other word. After children have placed the dots, reread the rhyme, asking children to check their answers. Have children replace any incorrectly-placed dots.

Nursery Rhyme Cover-Up

MATERIALS

nursery rhyme

sentence strips

markers

pocket chart

chart paper

transparent blue, green, and red Avery Dots (see page 61)

In advance, write each sentence from the emergent reader on a sentence strip. Write a sentence for each child, repeating sentences if necessary. Glue a felt strip to the back of one sentence strip. Read the emergent reader aloud two times. During the second read, point out capital letters that begin the sentences and punctuation that ends them. Explain that capital letters and punctuation are clues to where sentences begin and end. Display the sentence strip. Read the sentence aloud. Cut the sentence strip into words and rearrange the words out of order on a flannel board. Invite a volunteer to help you place the sentence in order and read it to you. Divide children into pairs. Give each child a sentence and a pair of scissors. Have each child read the sentence to his or her partner, and then cut it apart and mix it up. Ask children to place their partners' sentences in order. When sentences are rearranged, read the emergent read aloud again so children can check their work.

Cut It Up

MATERIALS

emergent reader

sentence strips

markers

felt strips

glue

flannel board

Reread It!

MATERIALS

big book
Reread It! signs (see page 61)

In advance, make a Reread It! sign for each child. Explain that everyone makes mistakes when they read. Ask children, *What do good readers do when they make a mistake?* Write student answers on the chalkboard. If not mentioned, explain that one way to correct reading mistakes is to go back and reread a sentence. Distribute a Reread It! sign to each child. Tell children you are going to read the big book aloud and make a mistake on every page. Explain that mistakes include stumbling over words, hesitating for a long time, or reading an incorrect word. Challenge children to quickly hold up their Reread It! signs when they catch you making a mistake. Read each sentence aloud slowly. Make a mistake on each page. When children hold up their signs, go back to the beginning of the sentence, reread it, and correct the mistake.

Using Pictures

MATERIALS

big book
flashlight

Ask children, *What can you do if you are reading and come to a word you don't know?* Have children brainstorm ideas. Explain that one way to check if you read a word correctly is to stop reading and look at a picture for clues. Ask a volunteer to stand next to you with a flashlight as you read the big book. Tell the volunteer that his or her job is to help you check your reading. Each time you stop to check your reading, he or she should shine the flashlight on a picture that will help you know if the word you read is correct. Read the first sentence in the book. Hesitate at a word (illustrated in the book), and then stop after reading it **correctly** and say, *Hmmm,* as if you are thinking. Wait for the child to shine the flashlight on the picture that represents the word. Say, *Oh good, I was right,* and continue reading the rest of the page. Choose another volunteer for the next page. This time, read a word **incorrectly**, and stop and say, *Wait a minute.* Wait for the child to shine the flashlight on the picture of the word you should have read. Say, *Oops!* and reread the sentence, interjecting the correct word. Continue the activity for each page.

In advance, write several sentences (with one or two challenging words) on adding-machine tape, such as *I get to eat lunch with the principal on Monday.* (Sentences can be taken from reading assignments, picture books, or emergent readers.) Tape sentences to the floor. Explain that one way to be a reading problem-solver is to stop when you get to a difficult word and look for little words inside it. Invite children to observe the sentences and read them silently. Invite a child to read the first sentence aloud. Before reading, tell the child to stop when he or she sees a difficult word *(principal)*. When the child comes to the difficult word, have him or her place a bracelet around little words (or chunks that sound like words) he or she sees *(princ* and *pal)* inside it. Help the child decode the word. Encourage the child to continue reading at a regular pace when he or she passes the difficult word. Continue the activity until all sentences have been read.

Lookin' for Little Words

MATERIALS

plastic bracelets

adding-machine tape

markers

masking tape

Discuss the cover of a nonfiction picture book. Walk children through the book, discussing each picture. Invite children to think about the topic and brainstorm words that might appear in the book. Record words on chart paper and read the list aloud. Explain that one way to avoid reading mistakes is to read the title and look at the pictures *before* you read, and guess words that might be in the sentences. Choose a volunteer. Read the first page aloud. Each time you read a word on the chart, have the volunteer place an Avery Dot next to the word. Repeat the activity with each page of the book. Discuss the story and congratulate the class on the number of words they predicted correctly.

Prior Knowledge

MATERIALS

nonfiction picture book

chart paper

markers

transparent Avery Dots (see page 61)

Oops!

MATERIALS

emergent reader

butcher paper

markers

tape

reading wands (see Magazine Word Bank activity, page 39)

In large print, write all sentences from an emergent reader on butcher paper. Number the sentences. Hang the paper on the wall. Read the emergent reader aloud. When reading, point to each word. Distribute a reading wand to each child. Tell children that one way to avoid making mistakes when reading aloud is to point under each word and make sure the word we say is the same as the written one. Invite a child to bring his or her reading wand to the butcher paper. Read the first sentence aloud. Invite the child to point his or her reading wand under each word as you read. Make a mistake when reading, replacing a correct word with an incorrect word. When you finish reading, ask the child to tell you the word you should have read. Have the child read the sentence correctly. Continue the activity with different sentences until every child has a turn.

1. We can eat the roots.
2. We can eat the stems.
3. We can eat the leaves.
4. We can eat the flowers.
e can eat the fruit.

Skip It!

MATERIALS

read-aloud picture book

construction paper

markers

In advance, write several sentences from a picture book on separate pieces of construction paper. Choose sentences with one difficult word, such as *Sam got a telescope to look at stars.* Ask children, *How can a person figure out hard words when he or she is reading?* Have children brainstorm responses. Explain that one way to figure out a word in a sentence is to skip it and read the rest of the words to see what makes sense. Place the first sentence on the floor. Invite a volunteer to read the sentence aloud, step on each word he or she reads, and jump across any word he or she does not know. Ask the child to consider the sentence and guess the word. If the child guesses incorrectly, ask him or her to consider the first letter of the unknown word. If the child still cannot figure out the word, have another child help him or her. Continue with other sentences until every child has a turn. Model the strategy with text, reading the book aloud, skipping difficult words, and going back to read them.

Sam got a telescope to see the stars.

WORKING
W • I • T • H
TeXt

Although most children interact with text even before starting school, they need constant reinforcement to increase their already-developing reading skills and love of reading. As children work with text, they become comfortable with it, developing into confident, independent readers.

READING SKILLS

Working with text develops the following reading skills. Children who understand and can work with text:

- understand print reads from top to bottom and left to right.
- know the correct way to hold and turn pages in books, understanding books have a front, back, top, and bottom.
- identify paragraphs by indentations.
- know text tells several ideas in combination.
- prepare themselves for maximum comprehension.
- understand what they read.
- choose books appropriate for their independent reading level.
- understand the connection between reading, writing, listening, and speaking.

TEACHING STRATEGIES

The following teaching strategies offer unique ways to help children gain text knowledge. Pages 80 through 94 provide dozens of text activities. Each activity incorporates the use of reading manipulatives and one of these teaching strategies.

- Use prediction and prior-knowledge activities to develop prereading strategies.
- "Play with" sentences, punctuation, and print to build an understanding of text structure.
- Use visual aids to develop comprehension.
- Work with and create text based on literature to demonstrate the reading/writing connection.
- Use finger plays and oral presentations to develop oral reading skills and fluency.

READING MANIPULATIVES

Pages 78 and 79 show several reading manipulatives featured in this and other chapters. Consult these pages when making manipulatives, when deciding which manipulatives to use, and to determine possible substitutions.

Featured Reading Manipulatives

Tell-a-Picture Microphones

Wrap a paper ball in cloth and tape the ends closed. Stuff the cloth end into a toilet-paper tube. Attach a piece of yarn with tape.

Floor T-Chart

Use masking tape on the floor, keeping it year-round.

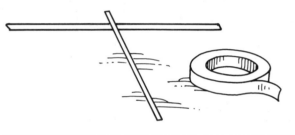

Correction Tape

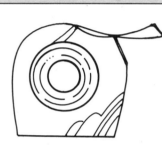

Know-It-All Mats

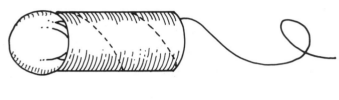

| language | location | customs | people |

Punctuation Makers

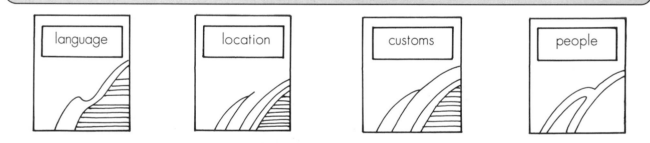

macaroni

quotation marks

comma/apostrophe

"O" cereal

period

spaghetti

Featured Reading Manipulatives

Magnetic Emergent Reader

Cut apart two emergent readers. Make one cut-apart book into a pile of even pages and one into a pile of odd pages. Place magnetic tape on the back of each page. (Two emergent readers are used so both even- and odd-numbered pages can be seen at the same time.)

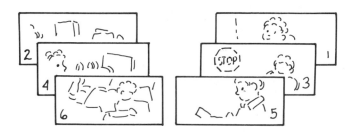

Floor Graph

Use masking tape on the floor to make a graph. Keep it year-round.

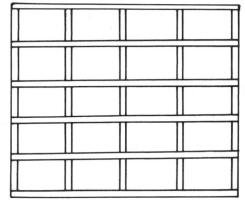

Good Guy, Bad Guy Signs

Tape construction paper circles to craft sticks. Write on signs with crayons or markers.

One-Line-Only Cards

Have children decorate index cards or cut-apart sentence strips.

Rebus Story Makers

rubber stamps   **stickers**   **magazine pictures**

Acetate Scratch Pads

Tape writing paper to cardboard. Cover and tape acetate to the cardboard.

writing paper

cardboard

acetate

What an Author!

MATERIALS

two picture books from a series, each written by the same author or author/illustrator

floor T-chart (see page 78)

index cards

Author Cards reproducible (page 137)

Reproduce a set of author cards. Make a floor T-chart. Label the left side of the chart *Similar* and the right *Different*. Explain that one way to make reading easier is to know about an author before you read. Tell children if they know what to expect from an author, reading his or her books will be easier. As a class, observe each picture and discuss the each book's characters. Have volunteers compare the characters and show their comparisons by placing each author card on the T-chart. Read both stories aloud. After reading, have the class read the chart and discuss its accuracy.

Tell a Picture

MATERIALS

big book and companion small books

Tell-a-Picture microphones (see page 78)

Make one microphone for every two students. Explain that one way to make reading easier is to observe all the pictures and learn about the story before reading. Use the big book to model how to "tell a picture." Point to the cover and hold up the microphone. Speak into the microphone and make a prediction about the story's plot based upon the cover illustration. Tell children they will take turns using a microphone and "telling a picture." Divide the class into pairs, distributing a small book and microphone to each. Have one child in each pair use the microphone and make a prediction for the first page. Ask children to take turns using the microphone and making predictions. Continue the activity until children have predicted the entire book. Read the big book aloud, inviting children to follow along in their small books to check their predictions.

The forest, the forest is home to a bear.

Cover a big-book cover with acetate. Explain that one way to make reading easier is to observe a book cover and learn about the story before opening the book. Have children observe the cover. Invite a volunteer to use red marker and underline the author's name. Ask children to tell what they know (if anything) about the author. Ask children to observe the book's cover illustration. Have children share their predictions about the plot. Have a volunteer underline the illustrator's name in blue marker. Ask children to observe and discuss what medium the illustrator used, such as pencil, pastels, or watercolors. Ask children to think about why the illustrator used that medium with questions such as *What kind of feeling did the illustrator want to give the reader?* Have a volunteer use green marker to circle the story's explanation on the front and/or back covers. Invite volunteers to read the information aloud. Have the class predict more about the story. Read the book aloud and discuss their predictions.

Reproduce the picture-book cover for each child. Tape construction paper over each cover illustration, displaying only the title. Explain that one way to make reading easier is to read a book's title and use it to make predictions about the story before you read. Distribute a book cover to each child. Have children read the title aloud with you. Have volunteers guess what the story might be about by its title. Invite each child to illustrate his or her prediction on the construction paper. (Remind children there is no right or wrong answer.) Invite each child to remove the construction paper and observe the cover illustration. Ask children if they are more convinced that their prediction is correct or if they want to change their prediction. Read the picture book aloud. Have children discuss their predictions and tell how they were similar to and different from the "real" book.

Cover to Cover

MATERIALS

big book

acetate

red, green, and blue markers

Titles

MATERIALS

unfamiliar picture book

construction paper

tape

crayons, markers

The Perfect Place to Read

MATERIALS

tape player

lively music cassette

chart paper

markers

Explain to children that one way to make reading easier is to create a "perfect place to read." Ask children to leave the classroom for 15 minutes and think about what you mean by a "perfect place to read." Tell children that when they return, it will be silent reading time. When children leave the room, clutter the classroom with books and papers, turn on lively music, and cover all comfortable furniture. Before bringing children in the room, explain that as they enter, you want them to look around and turn the classroom into a perfect place for silent reading. Help children transform the room. When the room is in order, discuss how the room (in its chaotic state) would have made silent reading difficult. Invite children to brainstorm conditions necessary for a perfect place to read, such as *no clutter, a quiet place,* and *a comfortable place to sit.* Post the chart, and have the class read silently.

Know-It-All Mats

MATERIALS

nonfiction books about countries

Know-It-All mats (see page 78)

old business cards

writing paper

pencils

In advance, acquire one book for every two children. Make one set of Know-It-All mats for every pair. Explain that one way to make reading easier is to record facts as you read. Divide the class into pairs. Distribute a book and set of Know-It-All mats to each pair. Have pairs take turns reading the book in class (or having their parents read the books aloud at home). As they read, ask children to write one-word or one-sentence facts on old business cards. Have pairs sort the cards onto their Know-It-All mats. Invite each pair to share their information with the class. Have children copy information from their mats onto paper. In future lessons, make other Know-It-All mats for other book subjects.

Gather an emergent reader for every two children. Use correction tape to remove all punctuation marks from the pages. Read aloud and discuss the story (without showing text). Divide the class into pairs. Distribute readers and punctuation makers. Read the story aloud again slowly without showing text. After each page, have children decide where punctuation should be placed. Invite children to make punctuation marks from punctuation makers by placing them on the text. Show each page of the story to reveal the correct marks. Have children check their work and rearrange punctuation makers so they match the actual text. Ask children to clear off punctuation makers before pages are turned.

Punctuation, Please!

MATERIALS

identical emergent readers

correction tape (see page 78)

punctuation makers (see page 78)

glue

Complete this activity with a small group. In advance, cut apart two emergent readers so both even and odd pages are "face up." Place the pages in a pile in random order. Explain that stories are written in a specific order so they make sense to the reader. Have the group spread the pages out on a table, read them, and place them in order so the story makes sense. Read the big book aloud. Have the group rearrange any misplaced pages as you read.

Sequencing

MATERIALS

two identical emergent readers

companion big book

Picture to Text

MATERIALS

magnetic emergent reader
(see page 79)

companion big book

construction paper

magnetic tape

magnet boards (see page 7)

Cut apart each emergent-reader page, separating pictures from text. Place text, in random order, on one magnet board. Place the pictures, in page order, on the other board. Invite a small group of children to read the text and look at the pictures. Challenge children to match the text with the pictures by moving corresponding text under each picture. Read the big book aloud. Invite children to check their answers and rearrange text if necessary. Place the materials in a learning center so children can practice again and again.

Fiction or Nonfiction?

MATERIALS

several fiction and nonfiction books

floor graph
(see page 79)

index cards

markers

Label the floor graph *Fiction* and *Nonfiction*. Explain the meaning of the words *fiction* and *nonfiction*, giving children examples of fictional and real things. Explain that books are classified as fiction and nonfiction—stories that give facts about real things and people are nonfiction; make-believe stories about "made-up" people and situations are fiction. Read the title of each book aloud. Invite children to discuss and decide if the book is fiction or nonfiction. Have volunteers write book titles on index cards and place them on the graph. Ask children to think about whether a book is fiction or nonfiction before they read it. For future lessons, have children use the graph to compare book genres.

Fiction	Nonfiction		
Mrs. Silly	Trucks		
Barney Bear	Whales		
Arthur			

In advance, make a list of several familiar good-guy and bad-guy book characters such as Jimmy from *The Day Jimmy's Boa Ate the Wash* or the wolf from *The Three Little Pigs*. Explain that, in many stories, there is a good guy (or gal) who tries to solve a problem and a bad guy (or gal) who creates a problem or tries to stop the good guy from succeeding. Have each child make a Good Guy, Bad Guy sign (see page 79). Read each character's name aloud, asking if he or she is a good guy or bad guy. Invite children to hold up their signs to show their opinion of the characters. Ask a volunteer to explain his or her decision. If opinions vary, discuss the character as a class and come to a consensus. Read the list until every character has been voted on and discussed. For future lessons, have children use their signs after you read aloud new picture books.

When studying a particular animal, distribute the same page of animal text and a Symbols reproducible to every two children. Explain that some books give factual information and do not tell stories. Discuss times when reading for information is necessary, such as when a person wants to learn how something works. Tell children a good way to read for information is to mark important ideas on the page (using removable markings if the book is not their own). Divide the class into pairs. Distribute a Symbols reproducible, three or four dots, and text to each pair. Explain each symbol, and as a class, choose three or four symbols with which to work. Have pairs read the text, write a chosen symbol on a dot, and place it next to corresponding text. Read the text aloud. Invite volunteers to share where they placed symbols. Have groups remove and replace dots if they made errors. Have children use the remaining symbols in future nonfiction animal lessons. Extension: Create other symbols and use them with different nonfiction text.

Good Guy, Bad Guy

MATERIALS

craft sticks

construction paper

glue

crayons, markers

Reading for Information

MATERIALS

Symbols reproducible (page 138)

page of nonfiction animal text

transparent Avery Dots (see page 61)

markers

The blue whale is the largest mammal. It can become over 100 feet long.

Floor Venn Diagram

MATERIALS

picture book with at least two main characters

index cards

markers

two long ropes

Read the picture book aloud and discuss the story. Lay two long ropes on the floor in the shape of a Venn diagram. Write the names of two story characters on index cards and place a card in each circle. Write *Both* on an index card and place it where the two circles intersect. Have children compare the characters and tell how they are alike and different. Write children's suggestions on index cards. Invite volunteers to place the cards in the appropriate sections of the diagram.

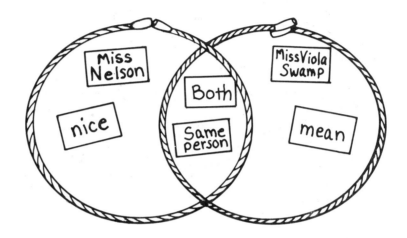

In-the-Book Story Map

MATERIALS

Story-Map Cards reproducible (page 139)

scissors

class set of emergent readers

tape

In advance, reproduce one set of Story-Map Cards for each child. Make a story-map answer key by taping Story-Map Cards on the matching emergent reader pages. Distribute an emergent reader to each child. Introduce the book and read it aloud two times. (Do not use the answer key when reading.) The second time, invite children to read aloud with you. Discuss the story. Distribute a set of Story-Map Cards, scissors, and tape to each child. Explain each term on the cards, and have children cut the cards apart. Ask children to reread their book and tape Story-Map Cards on book pages to show where each event in the story happens. To close, discuss the story elements and show the answer key. Invite children to rearrange misplaced cards.

Distribute a picture book to each child. Read it aloud, inviting children to follow along and look for descriptive words and phrases. Have each child find a partner. Ask partners to scan their books for descriptive words and phrases and build them with tangible letters. Have two pairs join together and share their words. Distribute Recording Charts and explain each chart category. Have children copy their words and phrases in the appropriate categories on the chart.

Feelings

Feelings

MATERIALS

class set of picture books with vivid descriptions

tangible letters (see page 24)

Recording Chart reproducible (page 140)

Have each child make a One-Line-Only card. To help children concentrate on each line of text, have them place the cards under the line being read and move it under the next line when the first line is complete. The cards help with fluency and are a perfect alternative to the finger sweep (moving the finger under each word) because they help children concentrate on a line of text rather than a word.

One Line Only

MATERIALS

One-Line-Only cards (see page 79)

instructional-reading text

Stump Your Partner

MATERIALS

big book

paper slips

pencils

Read the big book aloud. Provide each child with five paper slips. Have children think of questions about the story designed to stump a partner. Tell children questions about story content must be written on one side of the paper with answers on the back. Have children form groups of four. Have each group read their questions and answers and choose their five favorite questions. Then, have each child find a partner from the other group and ask him or her the chosen questions.

See It in Your Mind

MATERIALS

read-aloud picture book

modeling clay or dough

Introduce a picture book. Tell children one of the best ways to understand what they read is to see the story in their minds (visualize the story). To practice visualization, ask children to make pictures in their minds as you read a picture book aloud. Do not show the pictures. After reading, invite children to use modeling clay or dough to create their favorite scene or event from the story. Invite each child to explain his or her creation. Read the book aloud a second time, showing the pictures. Congratulate children on how their creations are similar to the book's illustrations.

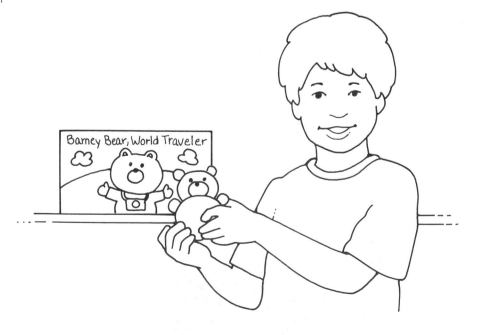

In advance, write *character, location,* and *time* on individual popsicle sticks. Make a class set of sticks and place them in a can. Read *The Three Bears* aloud and discuss the story. Have each child take a stick from the container. Tell children who chose *character* that they should change Goldilocks to a new character and rewrite the story. For example, if they replace Goldilocks with a mouse, the mouse might chew on Baby Bear's chair instead of breaking it. Tell children who chose *location* to keep the same characters, but change the setting from a house to another location and rewrite the story. Tell children who chose *time* to change the story so it takes place during a time in the past or future. Have children write their stories and share them with the class. (For younger children, use language experience, inviting children to dictate their stories for an adult to write down.)

Change It!

MATERIALS

any version of *The Three Bears*

popsicle sticks

markers

can

writing paper

pencils

In advance, choose a picture book with a theme such as sea life, healthy habits, or colonial times. Collect rebus story makers related to the picture book. Read the picture book aloud and discuss it. Create a word wall generating key vocabulary from the book. Distribute writing paper, story makers, pencils, and glue. Have children write words from the word wall and glue on story makers to write a rebus story about the theme. Have each child share his or her story. Display stories on a bulletin board.

Rebus Stories

MATERIALS

read-aloud picture book

rebus story makers (see page 79)

word wall (see page 42)

writing paper

pencils

glue

Class Summary

MATERIALS

picture book

red, green, and blue crayons

paper bag

posterboard

writing paper

pencils

Read the picture book aloud and discuss it. Explain that a summary is a short explanation of what happened in a story. Tell children that summaries give story events in order. Invite each child to choose a crayon from a paper bag. Divide children into groups depending on the color they chose, and give each group a piece of posterboard. Designate a writer for each group. Tell the red-crayon group to discuss the beginning of the story and have their writer write what happened. Tell the green-crayon group to discuss the middle of the story and have their writer write what happened. Tell the blue-crayon group to discuss the end of the story and have their writer write what happened. Bring the class together. Place the poster-board pieces next to each other and explain that together they make a summary. Invite each group to read their part of the summary aloud. Have children copy the summary on writing paper as a paragraph.

In the beginning of Jumanji, the kids find a game and start to play it.

In the middle, all kinds of wild animals and natural disasters ruin the house because of the game.

In the end, the boy wins the game and the kids set it outside.

Silent Discussion

MATERIALS

picture book

acetate scratch pads (see page 79)

overhead markers

Read a picture book aloud. Instead of discussing the story orally, have children discuss it silently with partners. Have children brainstorm ideas and words from the story and record them on the chalkboard. Divide the class into pairs and distribute one acetate scratch pad and marker to each pair. Have students use the words on the chalkboard to write a comment about the story on the scratch pad, and then pass the scratch pad and marker to their partners. Invite each partner to write and respond to his or her partner's comment, and then add his or her own comment about the story. Have children continue silent discussion until each partner has written at least three times. Invite volunteers to read their discussions aloud.

Read the picture book aloud two times. During the second reading, invite children to read aloud with you, emphasizing words or sentences that follow a predictable pattern, such as *But if you give a mouse a* _____ , *then he'll want a* _____ . Invite children to brainstorm how to change the story, keeping the predictable word or sentence pattern. Have children dictate the story to you as you write it on chart paper. Have the class brainstorm how to turn the story into a narrated, silently-acted play. Choose a narrator, actors, and set designers. Ask set designers to paint a sign on butcher paper showing the predictable word or sentence pattern from the story. Have narrators and actors practice the play. When performing, have set designers walk across the "stage" displaying the word- or sentence-pattern sign each time the pattern is read. Have the audience repeat the pattern with the narrator.

MATERIALS

read-aloud picture book with predictable word pattern

chart paper

markers

butcher paper

tempera paint, paintbrushes

costume and prop trunks (see page 7)

Display a picture of a different community helper or career in five locations throughout the classroom. Near each picture, place a marker and chart paper. Draw a line down the center of each chart to make two columns. Label the charts *Reads* on the left and *Writes* on the right. Over several days, read *Muggie Maggie* aloud and discuss it. During discussion, have children explain why reading and writing are important. Divide the class into five groups, having each group go to a picture. Ask groups to consider the pictures and decide how that person reads and writes on the job. Give groups five minutes to chart their ideas. At a signal, have groups rotate to another picture and chart new ideas under the previous group's writing. Have groups rotate to all pictures. Invite each group to share the chart information from their last rotation. Discuss the importance of reading and writing in "real" life. For future reading lessons, have children rotate to charts dealing with other book subjects.

On the Job

MATERIALS

Muggie Maggie by Beverly Cleary

pictures of community helpers or other careers

chart paper

markers

Cooking Directions

MATERIALS

easy-to-read recipes

cooking supplies and utensils

Each month, reproduce four copies of an easy-to-read recipe, and choose four children to become "head chefs." Explain that head chefs will read aloud and demonstrate a recipe so the class can prepare the food as described. Ask chefs to work together and practice making the recipe, dividing it into sections so each chef can demonstrate a portion for the class. Provide cooking supplies and give the head chefs a week to practice. On cooking day, distribute supplies to the class. Have head chefs teach the class how to make the recipe.

Reading Chain

MATERIALS

numbered sentences from a favorite story or poem

container

paper slips

markers

In advance, write each sentence from a favorite story or poem on paper slips and number each. Place sentences in a container. Explain that an important part of reading aloud is to read at a comfortable pace without long breaks between words and sentences. Tell children they will read one of their favorite stories together—their challenge being to read it aloud so it flows and is easy to understand. Have each child choose a sentence from the container. Ask each child to read his or her sentence silently and orally several times. Go around the room and help children read their sentences. Ask the child with sentence number one to read his or her sentence aloud. Have the child with sentence number two read immediately after. Continue the reading chain until everyone has read. Ask children how they could improve the reading. Invite children to read the story until it becomes fluent.

Distribute a picture book to each child. Read it aloud. Discuss parts of the story that could be dramatized with sound effects. Tell children that when reading aloud, it is important to read with expression so listeners can imagine the story is really happening. Choose a volunteer to read each story page. (When making selections, choose confident, proficient readers. The rest of the class will perform an equally fun and important function.) Give noisemakers to children who are not reading. Tell these children that they will make sound effects for the book using their noisemakers each time a "sound word" is read. As a class, practice reading and interjecting sound effects several times. Tape-record the final reading. Have the class listen to the recording and discuss why it is important to read with expression and how the sound effects enhance the text. Extension: Have children use body parts for sound effects, such as clapping hands for rain, knee slaps for knocking doors, or stomping for walking and running.

Tape-Recorded Reading

MATERIALS

class set of picture books with a variety of "sound words"

noisemakers (see page 6)

tape recorder

blank cassette tape

In advance, write a different animal name for each child on index cards. Place tangible letters in a container. Read *Q Is for Duck* aloud, inviting children to guess the answers on each page. Distribute Riddle reproducibles, and invite each child to choose an animal name and letter. Have children follow the pattern on the reproducible and insert their letter and word, following the pattern from *Q Is for Duck*. Have children cut apart the reproducible, glue each piece on the front and back of a piece of construction paper, and illustrate both sides. Have each child read his or her riddle for the class. Collect papers for a class book.

Riddle Book

MATERIALS

Q Is for Duck by Mary Elting and Michael Folsum

tangible letters (see page 24)

container

index cards

markers

Riddle reproducible (page 141)

construction paper

glue

crayons, markers

Finger Play

~~~~~~~~~

MATERIALS

Finger Play reproducible
(page 142)

old business cards

index cards

sentence strips

markers

class set of emergent readers

In advance, write the same letter on a class set of business cards, the same word (from an emergent reader) on a class set of index cards, and the same sentence (from an emergent reader) on a class set of sentence strips. Distribute a Finger Play reproducible, business card, index card, sentence strip, and emergent reader to each child. Teach the finger play. Have children read the finger play aloud, and use the props to perform it several times. Emphasize the importance of sounding like one voice when reading as a group. Close the activity by reading aloud and discussing the emergent reader. Have children find the letter, word, and sentence from the finger-play props in the book.

Something I Know

~~~~~~~~~

MATERIALS

index cards

pencils

objects from home,
brought in by students

Explain that one reason we read aloud is to give information to others. Tell children they will practice giving information through a demonstration. Have children think of one thing they can make or do (that can be demonstrated in class), such as make a peanut butter and jelly sandwich or drive a remote-control car. Distribute ten index cards to each child. Have children label cards *Step 1* through *Step 10.* As a homework assignment, have children take the cards home, perform the task, and work with a family member to write each step of the task on an index card. Have children bring the cards to school. Read each set of cards, helping children modify steps, if necessary. Have children sign up to present their demonstrations, spacing the demonstrations over several days. Invite children to bring in needed objects, read the cards, and show how to perform the task.

Tongue Twisters

Annie ate apples.

Buy black bananas.

Cute cats can crawl.

Don't dig daisies.

Eat eleven eels.

Fred found five frog feet.

Great green gorillas.

Help his horse.

Iggy imagined igloos in ice.

Jason jumped Jerry's jacks.

Kind kangaroos kissed.

Lily licked large lemon lollipops.

Mary moved my mittens.

Never nail nails.

Ollie owns our owl.

Purple people pick peaches.

Quiet, quick quails!

Renee read *Red Rubber Roses*.

Stop selling Sam's socks.

Ten trolls tell tales.

Use ugly umbrellas.

Vacuum Vicki's vest.

When would Wally wait?

Six ox mix a box.

Yellow yaks yawn.

Zip Zoe's zany zipper.

Book Page

Tongue Twister of the Week _____

Tongue Twister of the Week _____

Jump-Rope Rhyme

Name _____

Teddy Bear, Teddy Bear   turn around.

Teddy Bear, Teddy Bear   touch the ground.

Teddy Bear, Teddy Bear   turn out the lights.

Teddy Bear, Teddy Bear   say, *goodnight!*

Hokey Pokey

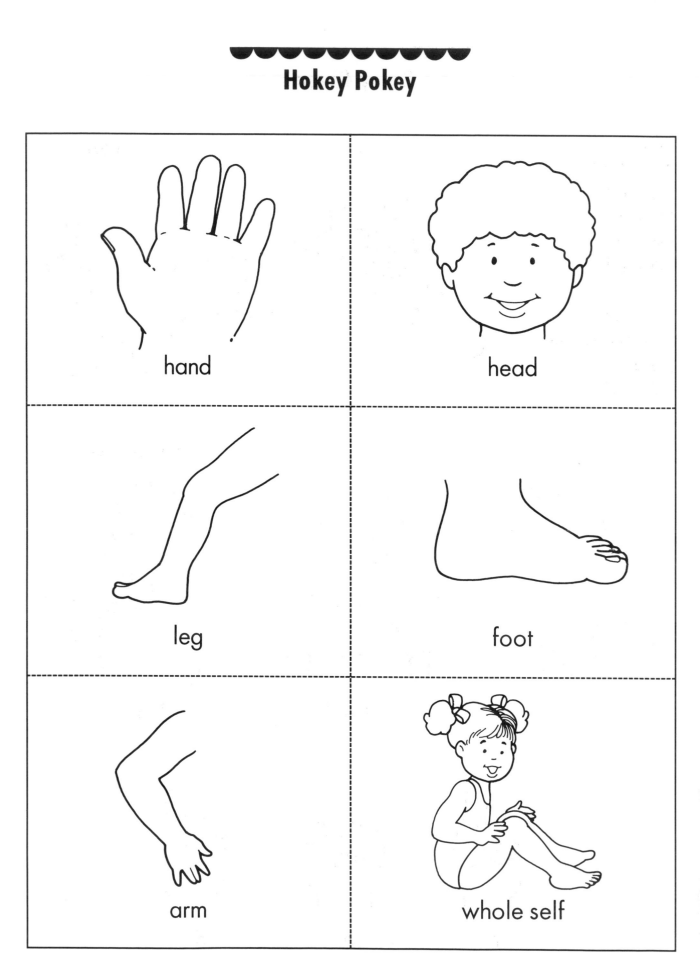

hand

head

leg

foot

arm

whole self

Developing Literacy Using Reading Manipulatives © 1997 Creative Teaching Press

Color Chants

RED

I like red.
I like red.
R-e-d
I like red.

I like apples.
I like strawberries.
R-e-d
I like red.

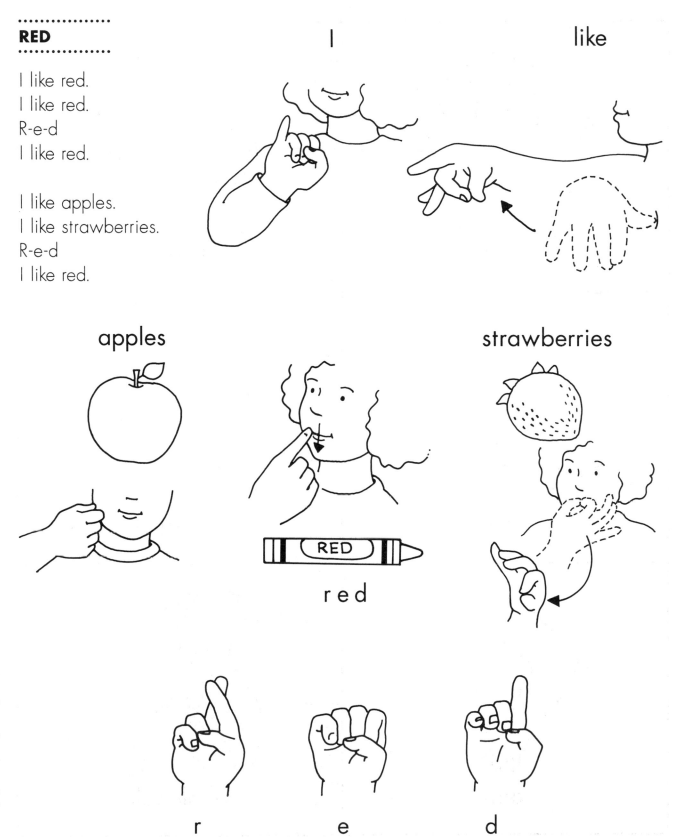

I

like

apples

strawberries

red

r   e   d

Color Chants

WHITE

I like white.
I like white.
W-h-i-t-e
I like white.

I like popcorn.
I like snow.
W-h-i-t-e
I like white.

I

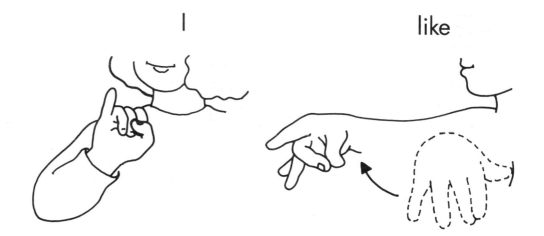

like

popcorn

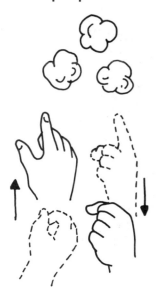

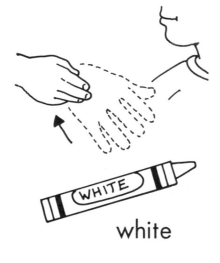

white

snow

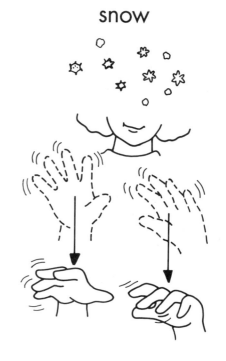

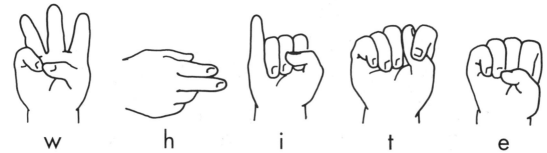

w h i t e

Color Chants

I like gray.
I like gray.
G-r-a-y
I like gray.

I like elephants.
I like mice.
G-r-a-y
I like gray.

I

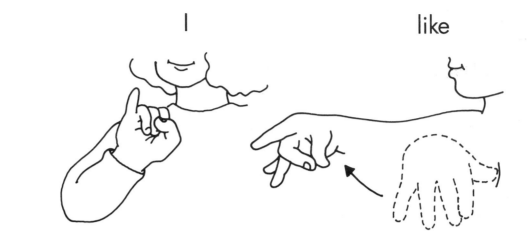

like

elephants

mice

gray

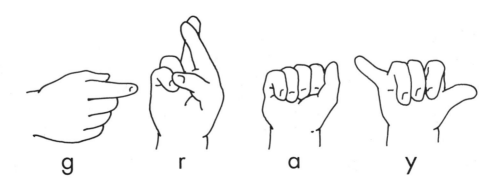

g   r   a   y

Developing Literacy Using Reading Manipulatives © 1997 Creative Teaching Press

Color Chants

BLACK

I like black.
I like black.
B-l-a-c-k
I like black.

I like bats.
I like spiders.
B-l-a-c-k
I like black.

I   like

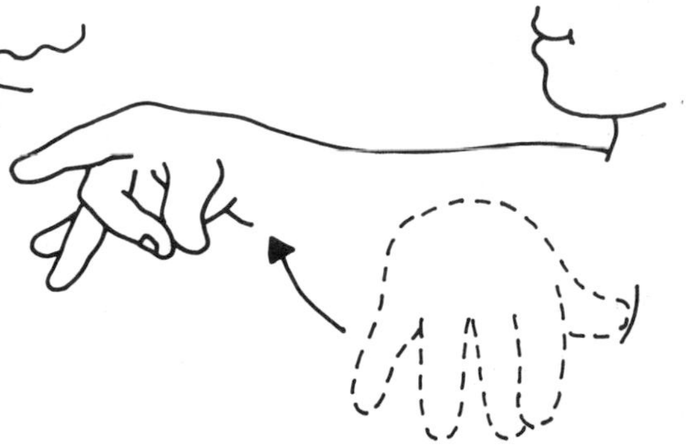

bats   black   spiders

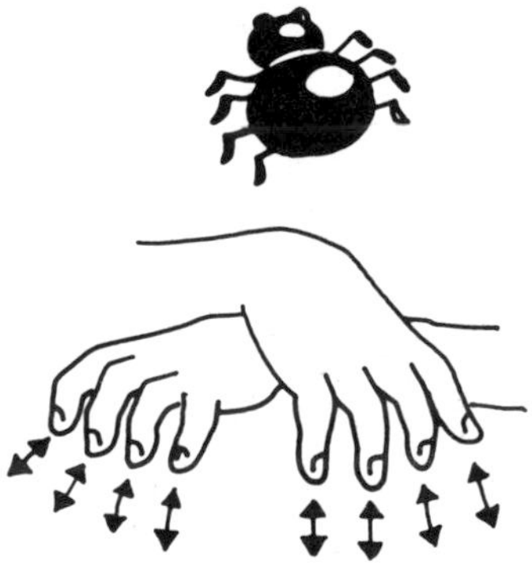

black

b   l   a   c   k

Color Chants

YELLOW

I like yellow.
I like yellow.
Y-e-l-l-o-w
I like yellow.

I like bananas.
I like the sun.
Y-e-l-l-o-w
I like yellow.

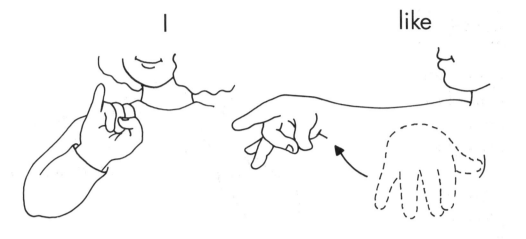

I

like

bananas

yellow

sun

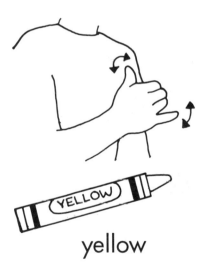

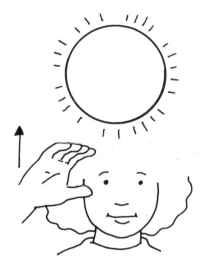

y   e   l   l   o   w

Color Chants

BLUE

I like blue.
I like blue.
B-l-u-e
I like blue.

I like blueberries.
I like bluebirds.
B-l-u-e
I like blue.

I

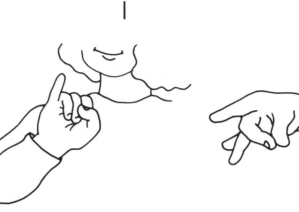

like

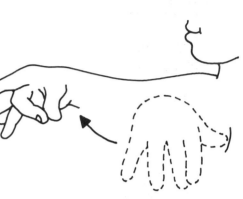

blueberries

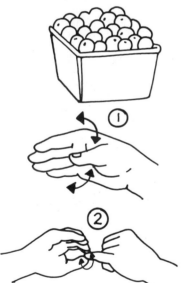

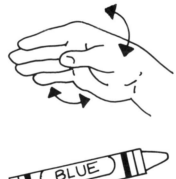

blue

bluebirds

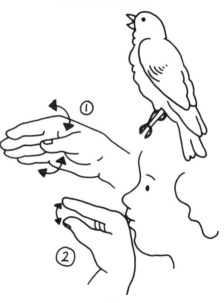

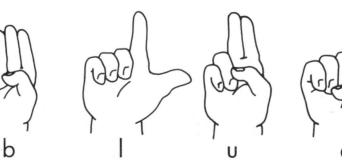

b   l   u   e

Color Chants

PINK

I like pink.
I like pink.
P-i-n-k
I like pink.

I like flowers.
I like balloons.
P-i-n-k
I like pink.

I

like

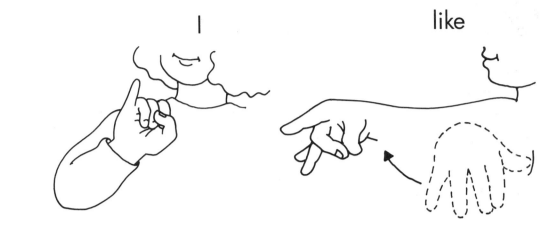

flowers

pink

balloons

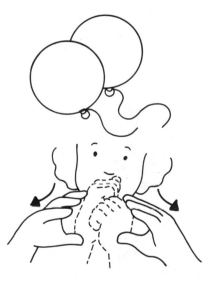

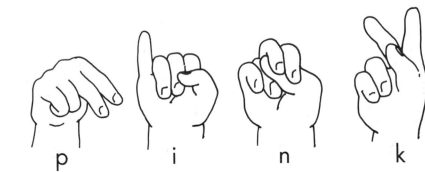

p   i   n   k

Color Chants

SILVER

I like silver.
I like silver.
S-i-l-v-e-r
I like silver.

I like nickels.
I like dimes.
S-i-l-v-e-r
I like silver.

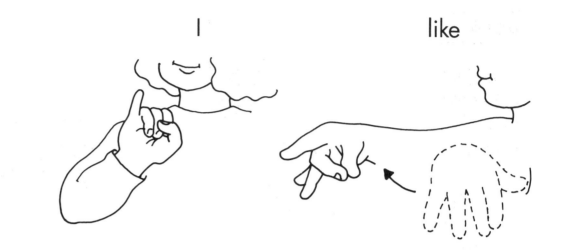

I   like

nickels

silver

dimes

s   i   l   v   e   r

Developing Literacy Using Reading Manipulatives © 1997 Creative Teaching Press

Color Chants

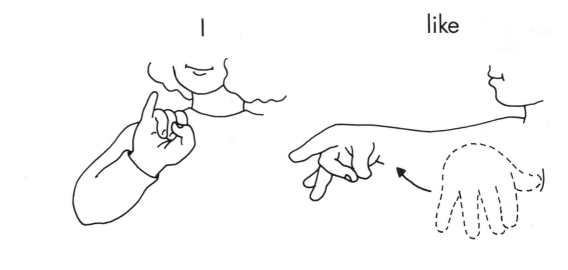

I   like

I like gold.
I like gold.
G-o-l-d
I like gold.

I like trophies.
I like rings.
G-o-l-d
I like gold.

trophies   rings

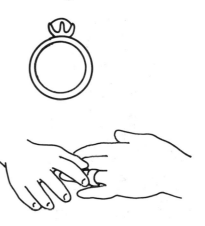

gold

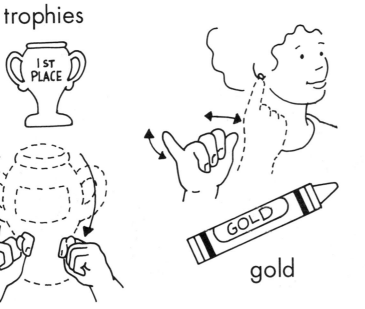

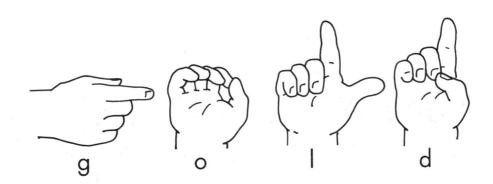

g   o   l   d

Color Chants

PURPLE

I like purple.
I like purple.
P-u-r-p-l-e
I like purple.

I like grapes.
I like popsicles.
P-u-r-p-l-e
I like purple.

I

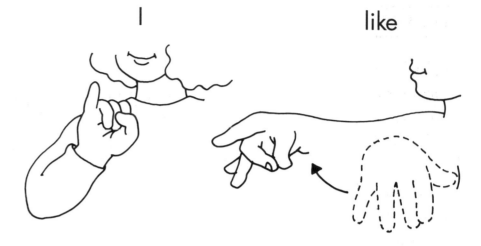

like

grapes

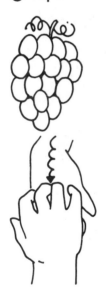

purple

popsicles

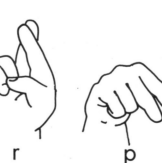

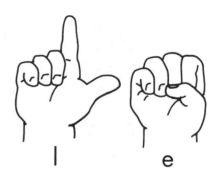

p   u   r   p   l   e

Developing Literacy Using Reading Manipulatives © 1997 Creative Teaching Press

Color Chants

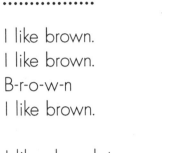

BROWN

I like brown.
I like brown.
B-r-o-w-n
I like brown.

I like chocolate.
I like bears.
B-r-o-w-n
I like brown.

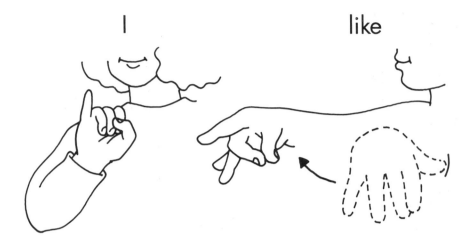

I

like

chocolate

bears

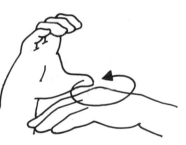

brown

b   r   o   w   n

Color Chants

I like orange.
I like orange.
O-r-a-n-g-e
I like orange.

I like pumpkins.
I like oranges.
O-r-a-n-g-e
I like orange.

I

like

pumpkins

oranges

orange

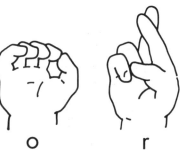
o

r

a

n

g

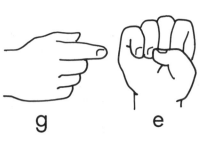
e

Developing Literacy Using Reading Manipulatives © 1997 Creative Teaching Press

Color Chants

GREEN

I like green.
I like green.
G-r-e-e-n
I like green.

I like grasshoppers.
I like caterpillars.
G-r-e-e-n
I like green.

I 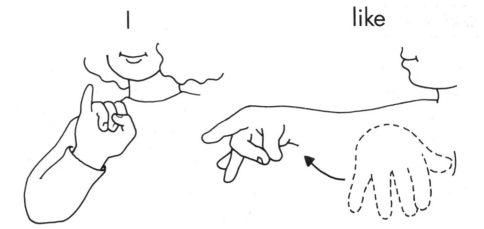 like

grasshoppers  caterpillars

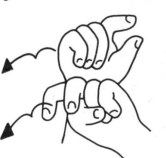 green

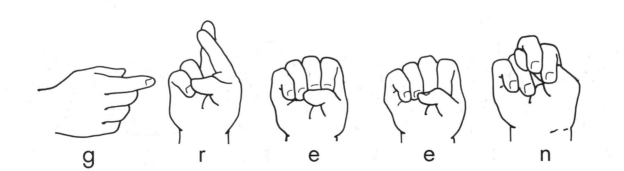

g   r   e   e   n

Other Ways to Use Color Chants

After implementing the Color Chants activity on page 18, use color chants in other ways. Create activities in which children

- match pictures to color-chant words.
- build new sentences from color-chant words.
- write stories using color-chant words.
- sort words by length and beginning and ending letters.
- make up new words for the color chants.
- play spelling games.
- use their names instead of colors and favorite objects instead of color objects.
- change verbs to other words such as *hate, love, hear, see,* and *feel.*
- substitute objects that rhyme with each color.
- create mini-books with illustrated chants.

Rhyming Pairs

tree

knee

tie

pie

cake

rake

box

fox

bug

rug

Fill the Blank

1 — pigs	1 — kings	1 — babies	1 — firefighters
2 — party	2 — movie	2 — baseball game	2 — grocery store
3 — tree	3 — giant	3 — house	3 — rock
4 — horse	4 — train	4 — rocket	4 — wagon

Developing Literacy Using Reading Manipulatives © 1997 Creative Teaching Press

Name-O Card

Name _____

Measuring Chart

Name _____

Letters A, B, C . . . (all capital letters)	Counters 1, 2, 3 . . .	Letters A, B, C . . . (one capital letter)	Counters 1, 2, 3 . . .

Pasta Graph

Name _____

Macaroni Only 	Spaghetti Only	Both

Sorting Rules

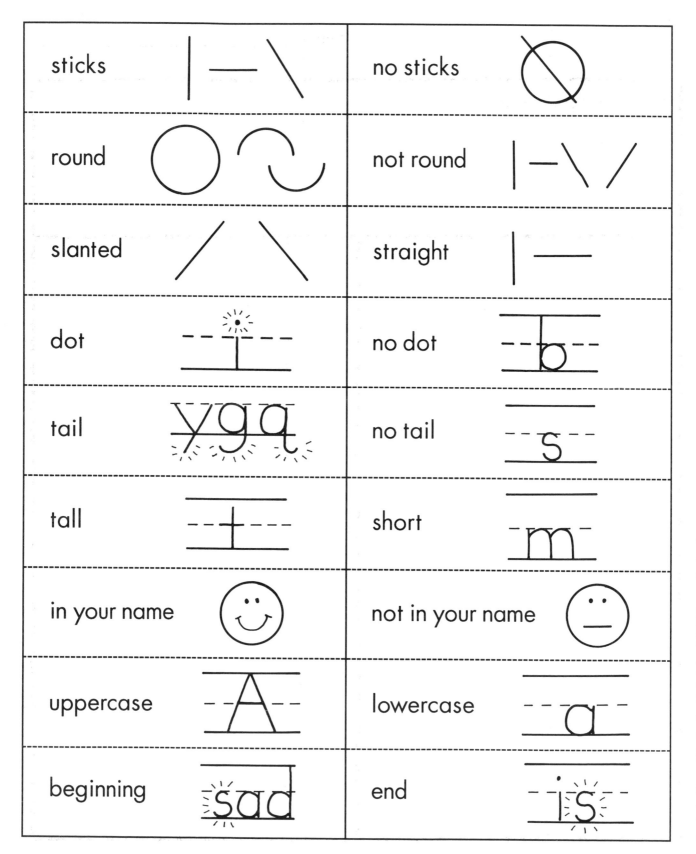

sticks		no sticks	
round		not round	
slanted		straight	
dot		no dot	
tail		no tail	
tall		short	
in your name		not in your name	
uppercase		lowercase	
beginning		end	

Developing Literacy Using Reading Manipulatives © 1997 Creative Teaching Press

T-Chart

Name _____

Place sorting rule here.	

Alphabet Line 1

Name _____

a	b	c	d	e	f

g	h	i	j	k	l

Alphabet Line 2

Name _____

m	n	o	p	q	r	s

t	u	v	w	x	y	z

Letter Set 1

Name _____

m

n

h

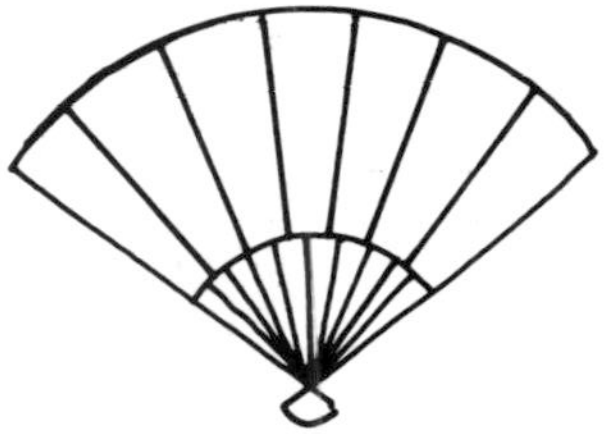

k

f

t

Developing Literacy Using Reading Manipulatives © 1997 Creative Teaching Press

Letter Set 2

Name _____

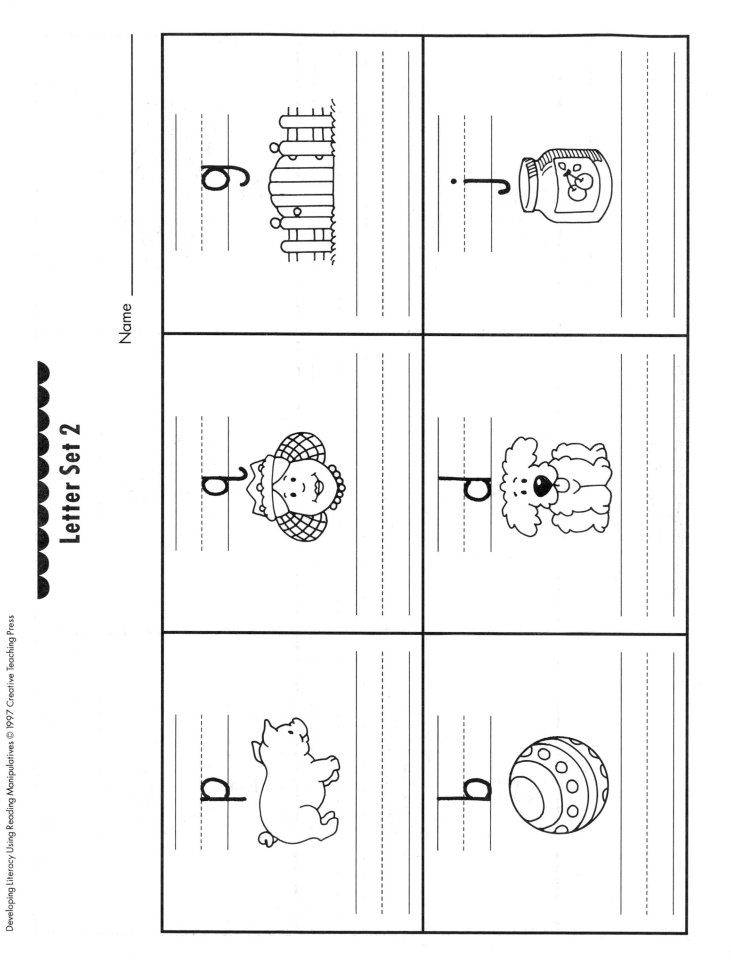

Picky the Puppet

Letter Card

Name _____

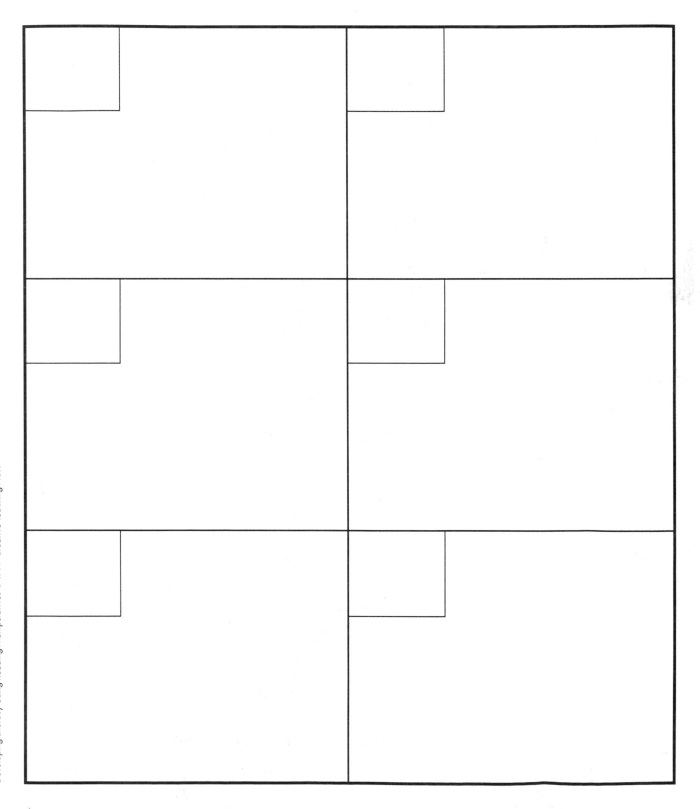

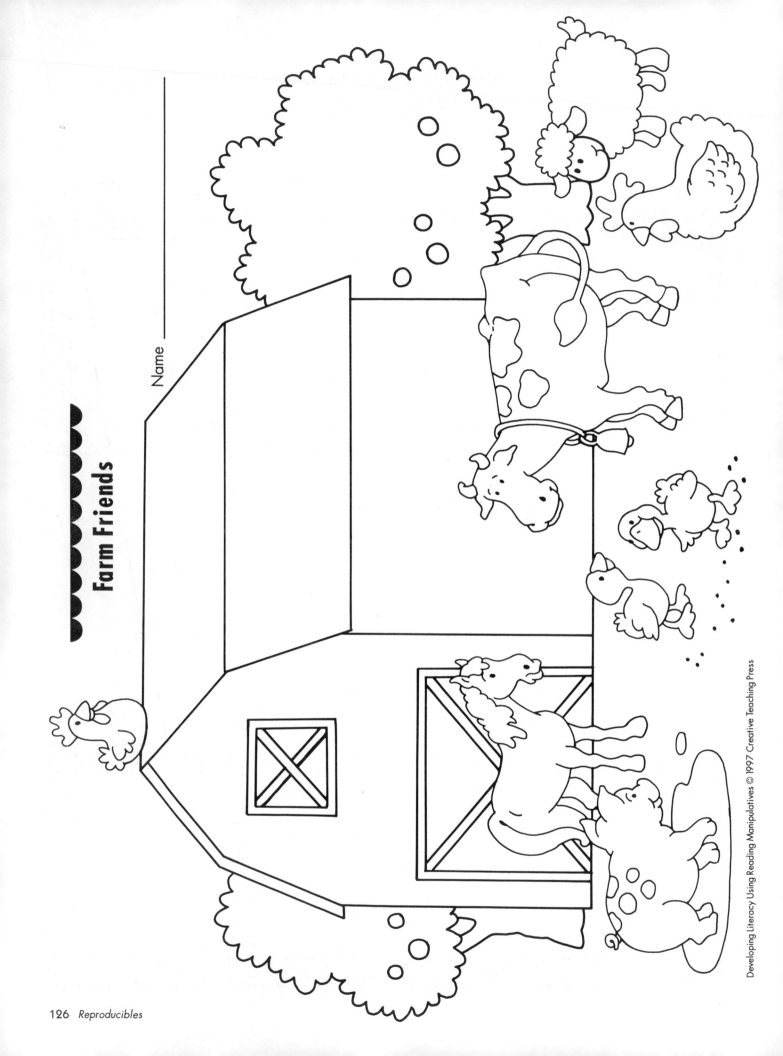

Name _____

Farm Friends

Developing Literacy Using Reading Manipulatives © 1997 Creative Teaching Press

Wand Words

Name _____

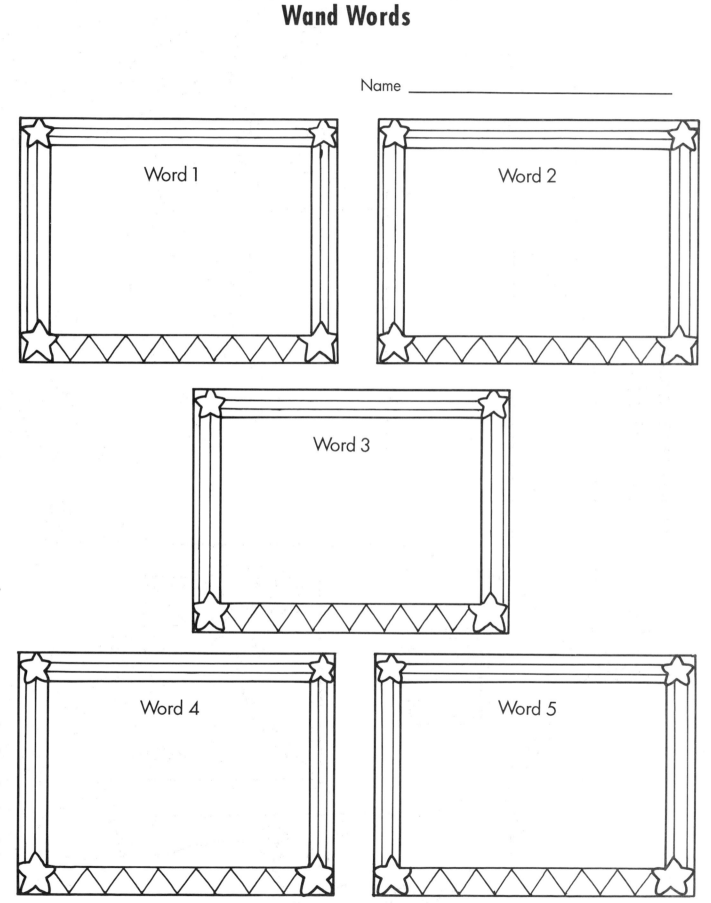

Word 1

Word 2

Word 3

Word 4

Word 5

Word Bingo

Card 1

Card 2

Developing Literacy Using Reading Manipulatives © 1997 Creative Teaching Press

I See Colors

by Rozanne Lanczak Williams

Name _____

....
COLOR KEY
....

green bead = *I*
red bead = *see*
blue bead = color words *(red, blue, yellow, green, orange, brown)*

I   see   red.

I   see   blue.

I   see   yellow.

I   see   green.

I   see   orange.

I   see   brown.

I   see   colors   all   around.

Humpty Dumpty

Humpty Dumpty

sat

on a wall.

Humpty Dumpty

had a great fall.

All the king's

horses

And all the king's

men

Couldn't put

Humpty

together again.

Word Pairs

cat	cat	cap	can
dad	pad	sip	sop
tall	tall	yell	sell
pen	pen	job	job
cry	try	red	red
wish	will	tree	tree

"Are You Sleeping?"

Are you sleeping?
Are you sleeping?
Brother John.
Brother John.

Morning bells are ringing.
Morning bells are ringing.
Ding, ding, dong.
Ding, ding, dong.

B-e-d bed
B-e-d bed
I spell bed.
I spell bed.

B-e-d bed, that's bed.
B-e-d bed, that's bed.
B-e-d
B-e-d

Developing Literacy Using Reading Manipulatives © 1997 Creative Teaching Press

red	brown
blue	black
green	white
purple	pink
orange	yellow

Bowling Score Sheet

Name _____

Frame 1	
Frame 2	
Frame 3	

Developing Literacy Using Reading Manipulatives © 1997 Creative Teaching Press

Sentence Makers

The	A	My	Her
This	brother	friend	horse
doll	baby	had	jumped
drove	ate	drew	carried
a	the	my	that
new	old	pretty	ugly
carrot.	dress.	eyes.	purse.
truck.	bed.	car.	pencil.

Watermelon Clues

1. I am bigger than your hand.

2. I am around all summer.

3. I love picnics.

4. I hold a lot of water.

5. I am heavy.

6. Most people like me.

7. My inside is red.

8. I grow up in less than a year.

9. I usually have seeds.

10. My cousin is a pumpkin.

Developing Literacy Using Reading Manipulatives © 1997 Creative Teaching Press

Author Cards

Age
(Young, Old, In Between?)

Gender
(Boys, Girls?)

Kind of Characters
(Animals, People, Other?)

Personalities
(Happy, Sad, Silly, Angry?)

Characters' Actions
(Good, Bad?)

Characters' Clothing
(Same Style,
Same Time in History?)

Symbols

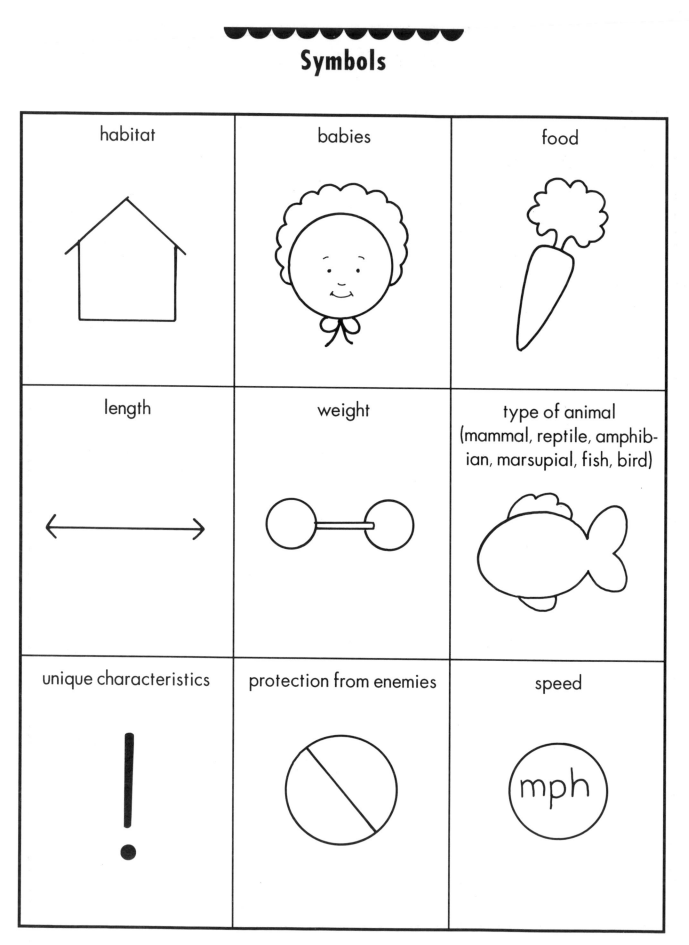

habitat	babies	food
length	weight	type of animal (mammal, reptile, amphibian, marsupial, fish, bird)
unique characteristics	protection from enemies	speed

Developing Literacy Using Reading Manipulatives © 1997 Creative Teaching Press

Story-Map Cards

| Introduction (Characters and Setting) | Main Event One | Main Event Two |
| Problem | Solution | Ending |

Recording Chart

Name _____

Character Words	Setting Words
Event Words	**Other Words**

Developing Literacy Using Reading Manipulatives © 1997 Creative Teaching Press

Riddle

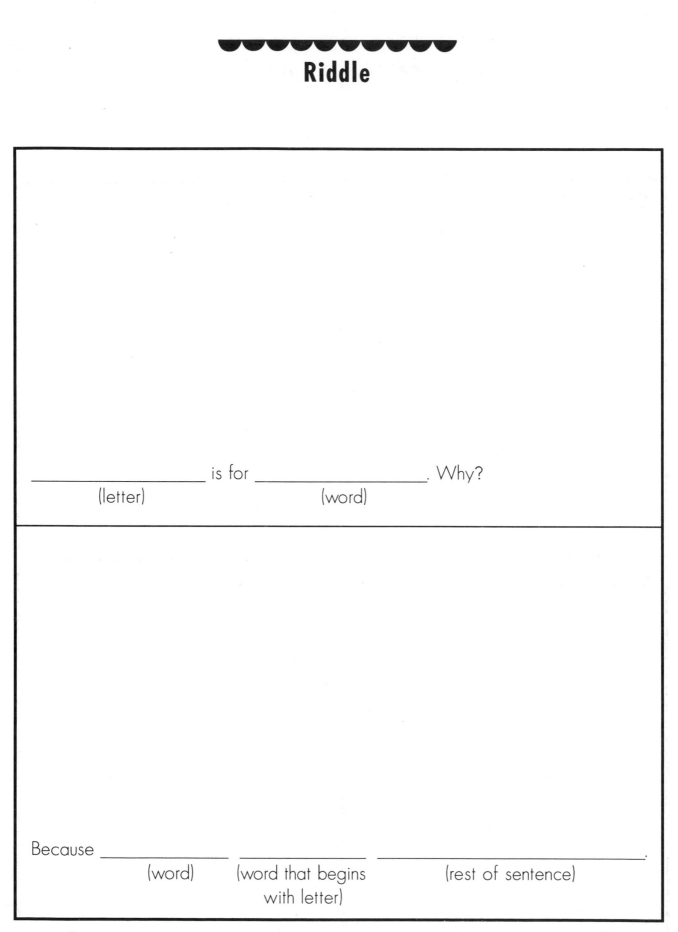

_____ is for _____. Why?
      (letter)   (word)

Because _____ _____ _____.
          (word)   (word that begins   (rest of sentence)
                        with letter)

Example: *R* is for **pigs**. Why? Because **pigs roll in the mud.**

Finger Play

Name _____

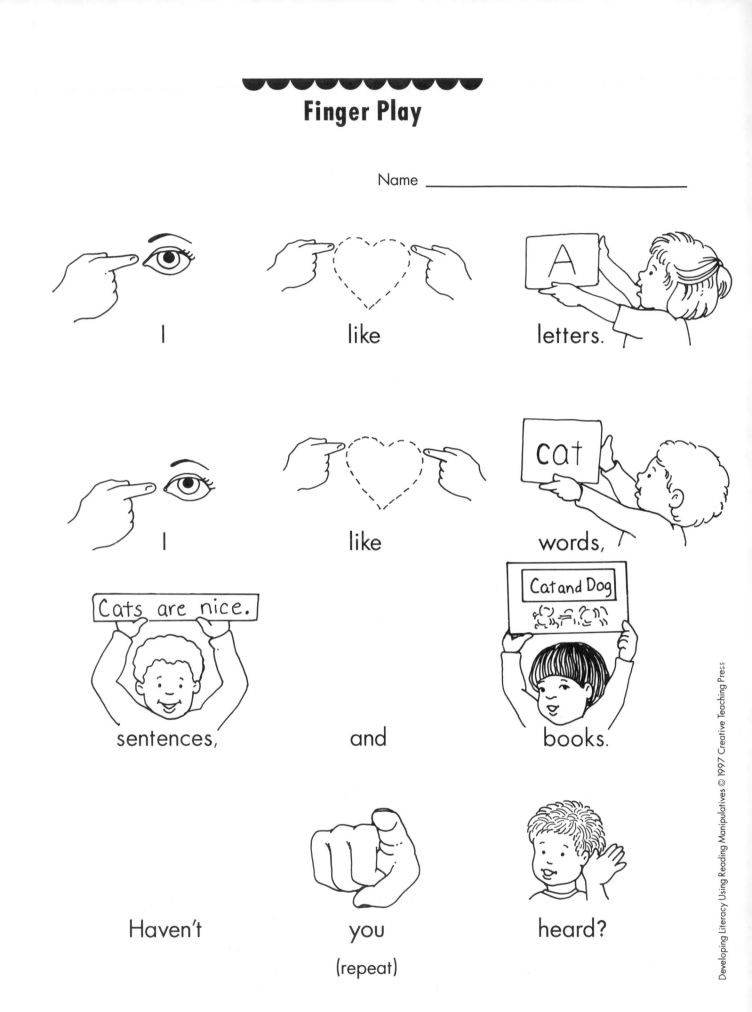

I   like   letters.

I   like   words,

sentences,   and   books.

Haven't   you   heard?

(repeat)